WALKING THROUGH WALLS
Practical Esoteric Psychology

Will Parfitt is an author, psychotherapist, Qabalist, relativist and poet. He has twenty years' experience of working with the esoteric, both at a personal level and in sessions with individuals and groups. He runs workshops and training seminars in practical aspects of esoteric psychology and has a private psychotherapy practice. He may be contacted via the publisher.

WALKING THROUGH WALLS

Practical Esoteric Psychology

Will Parfitt

ELEMENT BOOKS

First published 1990 by
Element Books Limited
Longmead, Shaftesbury, Dorset

Designed by Jenny Liddle
Cover design by Max Fairbrother
Typeset by Selectmove
Printed and bound by
Billings Ltd, Hylton Road, Worcester

British Library Cataloguing in Publication Data
Parfitt, Will
Walking through walls : practical esoteric psychology.
1. Esotericism
I. Title
135'.4

ISBN 1-85230-115-5

Dedicated to

A.B.S.

We are the bees of the invisible. We wildly collect the honey of the visible, to store it in the great golden hive of the invisible.

R.M. Rilke

CONTENTS

FIGURES

PREFACE

Secrets reserved for initiates are a thing of the past. No longer is the esoteric the reserve of a select few, a hierarchical group of people (often mostly men) who have some 'god given right' to be our 'secret chiefs' or 'hidden masters'. Every man and every woman is a star. We are all divine, not only in an abstract sense but in concrete, down-to-earth reality. The esoteric has become the exoteric and is for everyone.

The manifestation of this truth can be seen everywhere these days. From the Eastern traditions we have the 'secrets' of India presented by numerous gurus, the 'lore' of Tibet described in detail, 'sufis' in abundance, and meditation manuals and Chinese astrology available even on railway station bookstalls. From the generally less well known (or understood) Western Mystery Tradition, we can find workbooks on all aspects of magic, the tarot, runes, 'psychological astrology', ley lines, the 'secrets' of Atlantis and so forth. From further west we have Amerindian shamans sharing their world view with everyone who will listen, and even vast tomes on 'gnostic voodoo'. All this previously esoteric lore is for sale, and just as if you visited a different restaurant every night, you can sample a never-ending fare of the well-prepared and tasty or the thrown-together and bland.

There are two basic, common themes in these 'esoteric teachings'. The first is that each of us, as individuals, has the ability to change our lives for the better. We can connect with our spirit and find ways to become more in touch with unseen forces. We can learn 'secrets' that help us get more out of life. The second theme is that we are all interconnected – part of one family of life that is on the brink of a new age where all our collective planetary problems will be overcome (or transcended) and that through vibrating at a higher rate, being ministered to by angels or extraterrestrials, through meditating harmoniously, or living in some prescribed 'right way', we will be saved.

While I agree with the basic truth of these two themes, it also seems obvious to me that there is no easy way out. If we have the potential for this power and awareness, we have to work to manifest it. Reading books, visiting holy shrines, sitting at the feet of gurus, or attending endless growth groups might help us to find ways of manifesting our 'spirit', but it will not actually do it for us. We still have to do the work ourselves. Similarly, we can save our planet, and realise the beauty of the connection between all life forms, but again there is no easy solution. We have to awaken our inner awareness and see how each of our individual actions affects the whole. We have to re-own the power we have given away not only to politicians and multinational corporations and so on, but also to the teachers, shamans, gurus and 'trainers' and all the other 'New Age top dogs'.

Walking Through Walls presents a new view of esoteric psychology yet has its roots firmly embedded in the true Western Mystery Tradition. It can help each of us take control of our lives and become our own 'gods and goddesses'. No more hidden or manifest masters, no more looking, no more growing . . . just being who you are and doing what you do. You can become part of a wave of interconnected and free souls that will only be completely manifest when all living creatures are included, respected and given equal opportunity to be, do and become. It is not an easy road, but I hope *Walking Through Walls* will aid some of us to move a little further towards each other and perhaps discover we were never separate in the first place, and are always perfectly manifesting our soul's purpose at each and every moment.

DEFINITIONS

Many words in the English language can have different meanings, particularly those that refer to more abstract ideas or concepts. While there are no 'right' or 'wrong' definitions for such words as spirit and soul, those given here describe the meaning ascribed to some words in this book, and are intended to help your understanding. Ultimately, it is the meaning that is important, not the word used. If you prefer to utilise these words in different ways that is fine, so long as you are aware of the use to which I am putting them when you are reading this book.

esoteric   Pertaining to the *inside*; so 'esoteric teachings' are those originally meant only for the initiated, those inside a certain circle or group; refers to knowledge and understanding of the substance behind form, the inner truths we have within us that are usually hidden by the exoteric, outer appearance of things.

exoteric   Pertaining to the *outside*; so 'exoteric teachings' were those originally meant for everyone, therefore often considered commonplace; in this new age, what was previously considered esoteric is now equally exoteric in this sense; also refers to the outward appearance behind which inner truths can be discovered by the diligent seeker.

personality   Personal existence or identity; what makes someone distinctly themselves, their particular characteristics; that part of us which is comparatively exoteric, that is, visible, on the surface, of appearance; the vehicle for our manifestation, experience and expression, who we are in the world; and impermanent 'clothing' for the soul.

psychology   The science and art of the nature, functions and phenomena of the total human being which comprises spirit, soul and personality; the 'psyche' being the breath of life, the soul in all its manifestations.

soul   The essential, animating part of a person, the vital principle within each of us; the spirit is universal and is composed of innumerable individual souls, one of which can be found at the 'centre' of each living thing; each soul 'clothes itself' with a suitable form in which to incarnate; the soul, therefore, can be said to have a personality rather than a personality having a soul.

spirit   The total and undivided universal energy source out of which each soul individualises; often used as equivalent to soul, it is the essence beyond all forms and functions, including soul; it is totally inconceivable to the human mind except as a concept, yet is believed to be a living reality, an energy that both surrounds and pervades everything else.

· 1 ·

INTRODUCTION
Why Walk Through Walls?

Doubt is the only thing that gets in the way of anything and everything being possible . . . We can create our own reality with the only limitation being our perception of what reality is.

JACK LEE ROSENBERG

This book describes a new esoteric psychology which will not only enable you to walk through walls but is also fun to experience. Esoteric psychology does not have to be boring. Using this book, you will be able to have numerous exciting adventures which will stretch your boundaries and dismantle some of your old walls. You will be presented with a clear description of the worlds in which we all live. By coming to know and live more fully in these worlds, the meaning of your life will become clearer and your journey of inner and outer exploration will be advanced.

It is through your personality that you can experience and express transpersonal or spiritual energies. The more effectively you use your personality, the more clearly you are able to express your inner soul and contact those spiritual energies within you which can give you the power to walk through all the different kinds of walls you meet in life. These spiritual energies can also give you a happier and generally more fulfilled life. You can express the spiritual within you, not just in your creativity, but in everything you do. This is especially true of your relationships – both your inner relationship with yourself and your outer relationships with other people and your environment in general.

We can all become true vehicles for the love, life, liberty and light which are our true spiritual birthright. Each chapter of *Walking Through Walls* stresses the need for work on the personality, and offers many varied exercises for achieving the clarity such work brings. These exercises are adventures in both personal and spiritual growth. Enjoy these adventures, and realise that to discover more about yourself is always a great joy.

Each chapter also introduces spiritual aspects of the true esoteric psychology which is both original in its current formulation for the New Age, but also rooted in thousands of years of tradition. Reading this book, you will join in the traditional search ascribed through the ages to seekers after inner wisdom, understanding and knowledge.

As of yet most of us cannot walk through brick walls, or any other physically manifested walls. But we can walk through the physical walls we create inside ourselves – walls that keep us out of condition, fat, lazy, and full of poorly chosen food. We can also walk through the emotional and rational walls with which we have surrounded ourselves. And it is not impossible for us to breach the walls to spiritual energies which can then infuse our lives with purpose, meaning and positive, life-enhancing actions.

Most of our walls can be seen as being built upon distortions of various kinds. For example, there is the kind of distortion where you fall prey to a wall of illusion, living your life as if you are *just* a shopkeeper, writer, manager, lover, unkind person, sad person, and so on. You could have all these roles, and many more, but they are not the complete you, either singly or even in totality. There is the kind of distortion where you 'become attached to a wall', for instance being attached to a wall of illusion, believing things because you have been convinced they are true, such as that men are stronger than women, that you cannot do some particular thing you would like to be able to do, that the power of the state must be upheld, and so on. Any of these beliefs could be true: the problem arises when you believe in them whether they are true or not.

Walls can be based on passive fears. You might have a wall of body awareness that is distorted, where, for instance, fear really stops you from letting go and experiencing your body fully. You might have a wall of mental awareness that stops you experiencing some (or even all) of your emotions fully. Walls can be built upon some kind of 'reactive avoidance'. You might have a religious belief that tells you your body is bad, so you avoid it, and react negatively to representations of it, even in symbolic form; or you might avoid really experiencing a deep well of sorrow within you by always putting a wall of anger around yourself when you start approaching it. Wilhelm Reich said: 'Whenever natural, adequate, instinctive impulses are denied direct relationship to objects of the world, the result is anxiety, as the expression of crawling into oneself and the development of a wall of contactlessness.'

We need walls around us, but we are better off when our walls are semi-permeable membranes, so to speak, that allow the passage of those things – physical, emotional, mental or spiritual – we want to pass, and prevent the passage of those things we need to restrict. Without walls we could not be individuals. With too rigid walls, however, we can never fully connect either to other people or to the world around us. In either case – with no walls, or too many walls – we open ourselves to 'dis-ease' and negativity. In this book we will explore how we can honour those walls that serve us in some way, and learn to walk through those we no longer need.

When we savour the things of our world, we find in them our own inner riches. Everything we perceive about our world and the things in it are seen as if through an inner sensor. Maybe I do not always see what I want to see, but all the meaning in my world has been put there by me. What meaning has an apple unless I relate with it and see its red skin, imagine its juicy flesh and desire its sweet taste? What meaning is there in a beautiful work of art unless it gives pleasure to the observer and conveys a sense of its greatness? We choose the meanings we put on our world, and this book will attempt to teach you to put effective and joyous meaning on your world to enhance those things you like and which help you to become more fully yourself, and change those you dislike, using the transformative powers of love and will.

Whatever you think is either true, or can become true within the limits of the possibilities in which you believe. Extend those limits and what can become true is also extended. You can also forget all this if you so choose. You can invent limits, create illusion and fiction where you could choose reality and fact. You have the choice between war and peace, sickness and health, cruelty and kindness. We all have these same possibilities, carrying within us the seeds of all human qualities. The more we focus and act upon our own connection to possibility and the realisation of potential, the more people around us make similar connections. The more you are 'on track', the less chance there is of your inadvertently knocking someone off their track. You will find yourself more tuned in and able to withstand interference, conscious or unconscious, to your unfolding soul.

Transforming Our World

The dictionary describes the word 'transformation' as being derived from Latin *'trans'* which means 'across' and *'formare'* which means 'to form or shape'. Therefore transformation is change that cuts across and alters form. This form which is transformable is really everything of which you can be aware – appearance, character, disposition, nature, and all other attributes of an object or state, material or non-material.

> *If you look at some old wall covered with dirt, or the odd appearance of some stones, or some passing clouds, you may discover landscapes, battles, faces, attitudes . . .*
>
> LEONARDO DA VINCI

One form can reveal itself in an infinite number of ways. The universe is a projection of ourselves, an unreal image like a mirror that shows us only what we project. In so far as this is true, and we have no reason to doubt it, it can only be altered as we alter ourselves. If you want to change your world you have to change yourself. Another way of saying this is that we can never affect anything outside except as it is already inside us. We can change anything inside us, so, at least potentially, we can change anything outside us, too. It is not some mystical fantasy that whatever I do to another, I do to myself. It is a living reality.

It is of great importance that we connect to and use our abilities to transform our world. Many great artists and writers have attested to this truth. Franz Kafka said: 'A heavy downpour of rain. Stand and face the rain, let its steel rays pierce you, float in the water that waits to carry you with it, but hold fast all the same, just stand up straight and wait for the sudden and endless shining of the sun.'

We all have the ability to see something different from what we appear to be seeing, or, on the other hand, always to see the same in things that are different.

Believing In Yourself

You can only really go beyond a wall or block to your evolution and progress by passing through it. You have to be willing to take risks, and to believe in yourself. You can walk through walls by stepping forward with confidence, and being who you are. To do this effectively, you have to find a way of somehow unifying your consciousness with that of the wall. Then a transformation can take place and your relationship with the wall is changed. Like all unity you have the power to divide, and as you do this, cell by cell, you become yourself. You break the chain of separation by realising you are not separate. Everything you experience is part of you. Your power is limitless. Aleister Crowley summed this up well when he said: 'Man is ignorant of the nature of his own being and powers. Even his idea of his limitations is based on experience of the past. There is therefore no reason to assign theoretical limits to what he may be, or what he may do.'

How To Use The Exercises In This Book

To help you maximise the beneficial effects of any exercise in this book, always try to make sure you have enough time to complete it without being disturbed. Even if you can only spend a very short time on a particular exercise do set aside a specific period for it and stick to that.

Before starting an exercise, visualise yourself and the space you are using for the exercise as completely enclosed in a sphere of bright blue light.

Take up a comfortable position, either standing, sitting or lying as appropriate to the exercise, and with a straight but not rigid spine and closed eyes, take a few deep and slow breaths. Take your time doing this, you do not have to rush. Be aware that you are a unique individual choosing, at this very time, in this very space (that is, 'here and now') to perform this exercise.

Always take your time with an exercise – it is better to err on the side of slowness rather than rushing through it.

It may be necessary, particularly with a longer exercise, to read it through a few times to familiarise yourself with what you have to do. Do not begrudge this time, it will help you connect with the 'essence' of the exercise, and help you become focused. Some of the exercises could be recorded on a cassette tape, thus enabling repeated use of them without interruption. This is particularly useful for long visualisations. Alternatively, of course, you could work with someone else, alternating between roles of 'guide' and 'explorer'.

If you find any exercise particularly useful for you, stick to it for some time, even if you do not notice immediate results. Repetition of an exercise multiplies its power. Alternatively, if you find a particular exercise genuinely difficult, it may be better to leave it and return to it at another time. Do not worry if you find some of the concepts or exercises particularly difficult to understand. If this occurs you have to decide what is best for you – whether to move on to the next part of the book, perhaps deciding to return later to the difficult section, or whether for you it would be best to stick with it, using your personal power to work through this part. Whatever you decide, remember that walking through walls is fun. Do not treat yourself or the work too seriously. Humour is one of our greatest teachers.

It is always a good idea to record your experiences immediately after finishing with an exercise. It is useful to keep a record in the form of a diary or workbook. This may then:

- help you formulate more precisely what you know;
- increase your understanding and help you make choices;
- call into play your sense of values, and keep work in perspective;
- attune your mind to your intuitive processes and abstract mind;
- be an act of affirmation which strengthens your purpose;
- help you see long-term trends in your growth;
- aid your memory;
- record your successes and difficulties;
- help with many more things, depending upon how you use it.

This workbook will be for your benefit alone, being a record of you as you are and as you progress. Try not to censor or judge what you write. The more open and honest you are with yourself, the more open and honest you will become!

Finally, do not gossip about your work or prematurely share insights as this can often dissipate the energy.

How To Relax

At the beginning of most exercises in this book are the words 'relax and centre'. You can do this any way you choose, and throughout this book you will learn new techniques for both relaxing and centring yourself. The more relaxed you are the easier it will be to do the exercises, and the more you will get from them. You need to be able to relax both your mind and body to be in a fully relaxed state.

Relaxing the body can be achieved in many ways. Well known and effective is the technique whereby you relax each part of the body in turn, beginning with your toes and moving slowly up to the top of your head (or vice versa). By focusing awareness on each part of the body, feeling its tenseness, then consciously choosing to relax, you can work over the whole body and end up feeling very relaxed. Do not fall asleep, however!

Relaxing your mind is not always so easy. A fairly effective method is to imagine your mind full of the waves of a choppy sea which slowly becomes calmer and calmer until it is a still pool of water, untouched by any disturbances. Any thoughts that then arise can be allowed to send a ripple over the water but without disturbing its overriding serenity. You can devise other similar images to accomplish the same effect.

A good technique for overall relaxation is to suggest to yourself that you will relax in body and mind when you focus your attention on a symbol. You can choose any symbol for this – for example, a candle flame, a butterfly, a particular place you associate with relaxation, a falling leaf. Focus your attention on your breathing, then visualise your chosen symbol, knowing that focusing on it will bring relaxation. This auto-suggestive method of relaxation is very effective.

Simply paying attention to your breathing, watching the tide of breath entering and leaving your body, is another simple and effective way to relax. Some people aid their relaxation by focusing on their breathing in this way, then counting backwards from 10 to 1, affirming that they will be completely relaxed when they reach the number 1. This also works, but remember if you do this to count yourself back up to 10 when you finish your work.

Learning is finding out what you know already. Doing is demonstrating that you know it. Teaching is reminding others that they know just as well as you. You are all learners, doers, teachers.

RICHARD BACH

As you create everything you experience in your own world it is important to realise that if you argue for your limitations they will become true. Fortunately, the converse is also true! You can also create freedom of experience and expression for yourself, and extend this creation through your physical, emotional, mental and spiritual worlds. You are your best teacher, and using this book will help you come to understand this fully. Then you will be able to demonstrate your understanding, and remind others of their understanding too.

· 2 ·

THE ARENA OF EXISTENCE
Exploring Time and Space

*The natural depth of man is the whole of creation. Look at
the scope of yourself.*

WILSON VAN DUSEN

The base of all experience is in the senses, or more correctly,
'the act of sensing'. This applies to all the senses – taste, touch,
sight, hearing and smell. Experiencing is about sensing, and all
experience involves duality. Touch, for instance, can be tender
or hard, soft or strong, definite or indistinct, loving or hateful,
and so on. It may also, as far as our experience of it tells us,
transcend duality; you can touch someone with tender strength
or your touch might be light but convey much presence. When
you experience 'the act of touching', however, it is always you
doing it, and your choice how it is done. Your experience is
whatever you make it, either consciously or unconsciously. In
other words, you either know what you are doing or you do not.
This holds true for all the senses, not only touch. It is also equally
true of the whole arena of our existence. It used to be said that
'you are what you eat'. This is, of course, only partially true for
you are also what you experience in every other way, whether
spiritually, mentally, emotionally or physically.

You are not only what you experience, but also what you
express. The primary duality in the arena of existence is that
between experience and expression. You are either doing one,
the other or both. The basis for everything in life is our sense
of time and space. Nothing can exist except that it has space
in which to live. Try to imagine something without space and
it cannot exist, it cannot have a separate identity, whatever it
is. Or try to imagine something without time; even apparently
timeless moments only exist because other moments exist within
time. Without space there can be no matter, and without time

there can be no motion. All our experience and expression takes place in this space–time continuum.

The aim of the following exercise is to help you realise the totality of your experience through putting you in touch with the arena of existence. At first it may seem very simple – and that is true – but repeat the exercise several times so you really come to experience the meaning of this total arena, the basis for your total existence.

Relax and centre.

Look at something, anything in your surroundings, and realise it is part of your arena of existence. See how you experience it as being separate from you.

As you look at your chosen object realise it is part of what helps make you uniquely you.

Realise in this present moment, in this present space, you are simply yourself.

Continue looking at your chosen object, fully experiencing it as you do, while at the same time realising you are separate from this object. Your experience includes all duality and is beyond duality. You can be one with anything and yet separate at the same time.

The arena of existence is everything of which you are aware. It changes as you change either your awareness, your location or your time. It is often referred to as 'the ground'. We put structures on to this ground so we can experience them, as if they are reference points for our experience. These structures are often called 'figures'. Thus we have another primary duality – figure and ground.

For instance, as you read these words you might become hungry. From the ground emerges a new figure – the discomfort in your stomach. The figure becomes larger and stronger, brighter and more definite until it is your primary experience. You are no longer reading the words – you might be picturing the fruit pie in the kitchen which you made earlier, or you might be already on your way there! Whichever is the case, it will be true that these words will have lost their brightness and interest, and will have blended back into the ground. Hopefully, when your hunger is satisfied, you will then recall what you were reading and this book will become the figure again.

That is a very simple example, but try to realise how your total experience is a constant interaction between these figures – coming into and going out of consciousness, calling your attention and letting it go again. We might even have several figures demanding attention at the same time – this is often our experience – then we are thrown into a realm of disharmony or discord from whence we can only emerge by making a choice. Luckily for those figures you might not choose, choice is a threefold process – you can say yes or no to something, and you can also say 'not for now'. Listen here, stomach, you will have to wait until I get to the end of this chapter!

Nothing can distract from the arena of existence because everything you experience is part of it. You are wise, whenever possible, to attend to both the figures in your experience – which you will inevitably do – and also to the ground, which is often neglected. It becomes swamped, as it were, by the constant attention-seeking devices of the different figures who want us to fulfil their wishes. It is possible to try to get to the ground of experience by separating from figures, but it is generally more efficient to bring them with you. It is always possible to embrace a greater whole that includes both. The best starting point is always to attend to what is. What needs to happen will then spontaneously and naturally emerge, and will include your deeper and more meaningful experiences of the ground.

The arena of existence arises out of experiences. For example, a child's arena does not include the concept of inside and outside until it has that experience. Once structures are experienced and held they then crystallise and become 'real'. As this process continues, structures tend towards integration and coherence, where they are not separate from one another or from the ground. Once we are in the realm where this primary integration takes place, we often experience ourselves as being in an intermediate zone between the ground and figure, and our experiences are then distorted. We are open to fear – the fear of being separate or the fear of unwanted merging. We are mistrusting the process of ground and figure, and their natural emergence. We start imposing structures based on how we perceive things ought to be, rather than how they really are.

Fear and resistance separate you from the ground. If structure is made too definite and given pre-eminence over ground, then ground can become an obstruction, even seen as evil. A very definite and often very painful wall has been constructed. You are no longer able to be who you are, or experience what you experience. It is like not being able to see the wood for the trees. There is then a real need to orient to the ground and trust the process.

The next exercise helps you tune into the process of 'simply experiencing' and draws your attention to what stops you experiencing your inner process in its simplest form.

Relax and centre.

Sit in a chair and simply let whatever wants to emerge do just that. Don't do anything with it, don't censor or judge yourself, just be. Allow yourself to experience fully whatever emerges in your awareness.

As you do this, you will find your attention is broken; things happen which stop you fully experiencing the flow of emerging figures. Pay attention to these 'breaks', noting how they emerge, where they emerge from, how they affect you, how persistent they are, and how easily you can control them.

Structures tend to move towards integration and coherence, where they are not separate from one another or from the ground. As this occurs unconsciously, and without choice, it causes our boundaries and our sense of our self to blur and become indistinct. It is possible, however, for us to choose integration and coherence and consciously approach the experience of unity. We then reconstruct unity; it changes from something that takes us away from the arena of experience to something that helps us experience it in a positive, soul-enhancing way.

If you ask young children where they come from, where they were before they were born, they often give answers that in some way express unity, or at the very least an awareness of a larger arena of existence. Some children even appear to be mystics, pointing mysteriously to the sky and laughing! It is as if they know they came from some kind of a global undifferentiated state. As soon as they enter into their particular, individual, differentiated existence they join the journey we all travel, moving back throughout our life towards re-experiencing undifferentiated unity. It is the quality of the experiences we have on the way that will colour how we re-enter that state.

The move from unification to differentiation involves the building of walls. This includes those walls we construct of necessity, so we can be here in our world and experience it, and express ourselves as separate beings. It also includes those walls that separate us from our true birthright as separate beings who are differentiated individuals and yet still connected, one to another, and one to all.

Relax and centre.

Recall a valuable or desirable experience from your past. Allow yourself fully to see, hear and feel this experience.

What qualities were there in this experience? What differentiated it froom other experiences not so valuable or desirable?

Now recall a second experience that you value from your past. Again allow yourself to see, hear and feel this experience in the fullest way you possibly can.

What made this experience valuable?
How did it differ from a less desirable experience?

Focus your awareness on the similarities between these two experiences. Try to see how desirable experiences move you towards oneness, and reconnect you to the unity out of which you originally emerged.

The ground is always in the realm of the timeless, whereas figure or structure is experienced within time. The undifferentiated emerges into time and structure and becomes differentiated in order to have the chance to experience integration. Division exists in order that we may experience the reunification of love.

The ground must not be confused with the soul, it is the matrix for the experience of the soul. The soul experiences figures and ground simultaneously. Your individual identity integrates its experiences in the realm of time. The soul integrates its experiences simultaneously in time and timelessness. It is both transcendent and immanent.

Relax and centre.

Sit upright and simply allow your thoughts, feelings and senses to emerge. Do not do anything with the flow of awareness, just let it happen.

Then ask yourself: what are my resistances? What walls do I build which interrupt the flow of experience?

Allow yourself to experience the flow of awareness and the walls that block this awareness.

Bob experienced a wall that blocked his flow of awareness when one afternoon he was explaining how he always stopped himself just going with the flow. It suddenly dawned upon him how simple his wall was, and yet how subtle. There he was doing it again. Explaining! He experienced it more as a web than a wall, but it had the same effect. He saw himself as a spider, building this web around himself, stopping the free flow of information into and out of his awareness. He stated this condition quite simply: 'My web is explaining'.

What is your web?

Now once again watch your flow of awareness and each time you feel yourself interrupt it say to yourself: 'I don't know what is going to happen but I am not going to resist it'.

Connecting

Everything you experience, however you experience it, offers you the opportunity to grow. You are enriched by all your experiences. Perhaps we are alive just once, almost by accident as it were, and this one life is all we have. If this is true you might as well enjoy it as much as you can, be and do and become as much as is possible. You will not get another chance! Or perhaps you have a soul – the contention of this book is rather that souls have us! But either way, and whatever religious constructs we might or might not put on this, if there is more than just this one life, then the only logical, sensible reason for our having come into incarnation is to have the experiences of life. So whether you are a 'believer' or not, either way you are enriched by actions and events that foster your growth and you are stunted by those that go against your growth.

It has been suggested that all living creatures live within a collective ocean of experience. Perhaps animals and plants live in this 'ocean' all the time, and, by nature of our thinking about ourselves and our separate identity, and then our getting trapped into believing this is all we are, perhaps we humans are the only living creatures who are separate from this ocean of experience. If we can return to this total arena of existence, where we do not experience ourselves as separate, but part of the whole planetary consciousness, we can grow in a way that always enhances not only ourselves but all sentient beings. Even if this is a fantasy, an illusion, even if we are just an accident of evolution, why should we not try to make it happen, make it the truth? We have the power to be, do and become everything and anything we want.

We will not attain this or any other desirable, growthful experience by trying to get there, as if it is somewhere we need to go. There is nowhere we can travel to find ourselves. To bridge the gulf between our separate and insignificant existence, and that of a connected and significant existence we have to transform what is inside. Then we truly grow.

If you kick a ball you can either think that you caused an effect, that is, kicked the ball, or you can think that both you and the ball were both effects of a larger cause. With such a trivial example you may ask what is the difference? But consider the same distinction if applied to a more important action – for example, your political and social actions. You have a clear choice: to be disconnected and in a dream, within an illusion of separation, or connected and awake.

When you are connected and awake you are then able to 'see' rather than just look, 'listen' rather than just hear, 'feel' rather than just touch. Your connections then draw to you what Carl Jung termed synchronicities – events that happen simultaneously as if not through coincidence, but as if connected by some larger agent of truth and harmony. This is the soul, which works through you to make these things happen.

You might then start seeing, for example, 'teachings' from unusual or unexpected sources. Guy was feeling very run down and depressed after his girlfriend and he had an argument and she went to stay with a friend. He felt disconnected from everyone and everything. He started meditating and working on his process but found it a really difficult, uphill struggle. It was much easier to turn on the television and go into a deadening trance. Then one day he was watching 'Star Trek' and Captain Kirk said, while holding someone's hand, that, man or woman, it does not matter, we are all humans, littles pieces of flesh and blood afloat in an endless universe and all we have, that we can hold on to, is our fellow humans. This 'direct message' rang a bell in Guy's consciousness; he realised in a really deep way the truth of this statement. He phoned his girlfriend, shared his insight with her, and they began to work on renewing their relationship.

Outer and Inner Intelligence

Outer or 'lower' intelligence is the ordering of information. It is putting structure on to what we experience. It takes place primarily in the left part of the brain. Inner or 'higher' intelligence is making connections between items of information and is primarily a function of the right part of the brain.

An example of outer intelligence might be discovering that it is possible to be in a relationship without experiencing jealousy. Inner intelligence would then be connecting this discovery to your own relationship and acting upon it. Outer intelligence has been described as knowledge, while inner intelligence is more akin to understanding. Knowledge without understanding is always partial and often sterile. True intelligence is increased through the discovery and utilisation of better methods for both ordering and connecting information.

The 'god' or energy described by the name 'Prometheus' is usually described as a being who learned to bring fire down from heaven. We can learn a lot from his story. In Greek Prometheus means 'fore-thought' ('pro' = fore + 'methius' = thought). This forethought really refers to the forebrain, the cerebellum, which when it developed sufficiently in humans over the older, animal brain (the hindbrain), gave us the ability to 'steal' fire from heaven.

So how can we steal fire from heaven, or to put it another way, become inspired? What is this forethought that happens in our forebrain? The dictionary describes it as 'previous thinking' or devising deliberate intention, and care for the future. By stealing fire from heaven, the forebrain allows the human to make creative connections that were previously impossible. Thinking is ascribed to the element of air in the traditional 'elements of the wise', that is, fire, water, air and earth. Forethought adds, as it were, creativity (fire) to the air the human already has.

The myth of Prometheus says he utilised water and earth to create humans. If we add his fire (creative forethought) and air (ordinary thinking) to these two elements, we see him using all the four elements to create the human race as we know it. In the process of this creation he gave to humanity all the qualities possessed by other animals through adding to rather than replacing the older brain.

Zeus was angry at Prometheus's actions so chained him to a rock and an eagle was sent every day to consume his liver (=soul). This was then restored each succeeding night. That is to say, he entered into a cycle of incarnations (for day/night = life/death). Hercules, the strongest of the humans he had created, killed the eagle and delivered his creator. Hercules represents human strength and cunning, and development – having reached a stage where he was no longer chained to the wheel of life and death. Then Chiron (who was a wise magician from the pre-human race of centaurs with skills in medicine, music and prophecy) gave him his immortality. Humans were then accepted as being equal to the gods.

Your task, as presented throughout the rest of this book, is to become as strong as Hercules so you too can 'kill' the eagle of illusion. You can do this through modelling the behaviour of Prometheus. This involves bringing fire from heaven (having creative forethought), using your air (formative thinking functions) and your water (feelings and emotional understanding) to really manifest your soul in the realm of manifestation, the earth. You will then be using the four elements of the wise which, combined with the strength and growth of Hercules, turns us into gods and goddesses in our lives, able to direct and change our lives effectively in a way that satisfies the needs of the soul which we have incarnated to develop.

· 3 ·

FINDING YOUR WAY
Exploring Consciousness

*If you wish to know the way up a mountain, you must ask
the person who goes back and forth on it.*

R. H. BLYTH

For someone to show you the way to be, do or become anything,
they already have to have the knowledge and experience of that
way themselves. A mountain guide who had never been on the
mountain would not get many customers. A person who wishes
to be a good guide – whether it is to mountains, consciousness or
anything else – needs to be constantly exploring themself, going
to the limits of their existing knowledge and experience, and
stretching it that little bit further each time. Then when he or
she leads other people along the way, the guide can be confident
about what will be met as they move on.

Similarly, whether experienced or not, a guide who pushes
his clients up the mountain, or one who drags them along, not
letting them travel at their own pace, will not be doing the
job efficiently. It might be very appropriate to stretch people
to the very edge of their ability, but to push them too far (or
not take them far enough) will be of little use to them or the
guide.

Whether you travel with a guide or choose to journey alone,
it is important to have a map. It seems almost unnecessary to
stress the importance of having good maps. An out-of-date
map of Tasmania is of little use to you if you are travelling
in modern-day Spain! Likewise, an out-of-date map of human
consciousness will also be of little use to a modern-day traveller.
A good map helps you to see where you are, and your relationship to both where you have come from (the past) and where
you are travelling to (the future). It will help you to see who you
are, particularly as it focuses you on to your present moment in

both time and space; that is, as it brings you closer to a true experience of the here and now.

The very best maps can also act as guidebooks. At the very least you need a guide to the symbols on the map. Without it how would you know, for example, that a little black circle with a cross above it is a church with a spire? More than that, however, you need to be able to read the map effectively, and a good guidebook will offer this information. It will also cover some of the other factors you need to know on your journey – local colour to help you really appreciate where you are.

The better the guidebook the more able you are to follow the Rosicrucian adage to 'wear the cloth of the country in which you are travelling'. This does not mean the same as 'when in Rome do as the Romans do'. On the contrary, it is of vital importance, wherever you travel inside or outside of your own consciousness, to be yourself. But when you travel in unknown or new places, it is well worth remembering to wear the appropriate gear. A mountain climber in a bikini and flip-flops cuts a ridiculous figure! Merely having an uncovered head might get you attacked if you were to go that way into a religious shrine in some places.

There are three maps which also serve as excellent guidebooks to travels within the realms of consciousness. They are quite different maps, but all three of them offer really useful information for the explorer of the Self. You might prefer one to the others, or wish to use all three, or you might find another map that suits you better. Whatever is the case for you, remember, finally, that the map is most definitely not the territory. It is a static version of a dynamic reality. It is not the truth, but a representation of it. It is, however, a useful tool for facilitating our inner exploration.

When you get right down to it, and are 'out there' exploring yourself, you have to really experience the territory, to become fully involved in the experiences you are having. Thus it is well worth spending some time studying these guidebooks so that when you are actively travelling – climbing a psychological mountain, bridging an emotional river, dismantling a spiritual wall, whatever – you are helped through your familiarity with the territory.

The Egg of Being

'The Egg of Being' is the main map used by psychosynthesis. Psychosynthesis is a psychological system devised in Italy in the early to mid-twentieth century by Roberto Assagioli. Psychosynthesis is more than just a theory, it is a practical working method that incorporates many approaches to personal growth. These methods are unified around the self (or 'I') which is seen as the core of each individual. This self can direct the harmonious development of all aspects of the personality. Beyond this personal harmony lie higher realms of creativity and spiritual experience.

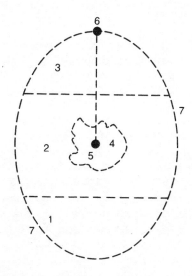

Figure 1: The Egg of Being

It is an artificial division, but to help our understanding, psychosynthesis makes a distinction between two realms – the personal and the transpersonal (or spiritual). These two realms are interwoven, they proceed together and are truly indivisible. Personal psychosynthesis concentrates on building a personality that is effective and relatively free from walls of any kind, is able to direct its energies constructively, and have a clear awareness of its own centre. Spiritual psychosynthesis explores the transpersonal regions, areas beyond everyday awareness such as the source of intuition, creative imagination, states of illumination, and the sense of value or meaning in life. Its exploration culminates in the discovery of the Higher Self, our true essence beyond all masks and conditioning.

The 'egg of being' represents our total psyche. The three horizontal divisions of the egg stand for past (1), present (2) and future (3). All three are constantly active within us, although in different ways.

1. Represents the lower unconscious, our personal psychological past including repressed complexes and long-forgotten memories, instincts, and physical functions over which we (usually) have no conscious control.

2. Represents the middle unconscious, the place where all states of mind reside, which can be brought at will into our field of consciousness (4). In our version of the psychosynthesis egg it is shaped like an amoeba to show how it is constantly changing as our chosen field of awareness changes.

3. Represents the superconscious, our evolutionary future, where we are going, the region from where we receive our higher inspirations and intuitions – artistic, philosophical or scientific, however they are experienced.

The exploration of these three realms is one of the main tasks of psychosynthesis. The distinction between 'higher' or 'super'-conscious and 'lower' unconscious is developmental, not moralistic. The lower unconscious is not bad, just earlier in our evolution. The superconscious is not merely an abstract possibility but a living reality with an existence of its own.

5. Is the personal self, our individual 'I' who experiences all this. It is the 'I' that experiences itself as having thoughts, feelings and sensations. This personal self is a reflection or spark of (6), the spiritual Self which is both universal and individual in nature. Note how it is half inside and half outside the egg. The realisation of this 'transpersonal' Self is a mark of spiritual fulfilment.

7. Represents the collective unconscious that is common to all living beings. Note how in the egg the lines are dotted to

show that there are no rigid compartments to impede free interplay between all these 'levels' of unconsciousness.

Circuits of Living

The map or guidebook called 'Circuits of Living' was developed by Timothy Leary and Robert Anton Wilson in particular. Their work was based on their own personal explorations of the psyche and the work done by inner explorers such as George Gurdjieff.

The two tables (pp. 28 and 29) show the scheme of this map which is based upon eight circuits or 'systems' which describe the whole of consciousness, including both what is and what can be. The best way to understand this guidebook is to study these tables and read the following notes on the different circuits.

Circuits 1 to 4 are 'terrestrial' in nature, they describe what exists within earthbound consciousness. They are generated by and connected to the left lobe of the brain and all are present in the individual, in either a clear or more or less distorted way.

Circuits 5 to 8 describe the future evolution of consciousness. They are connected with the right lobe of the brain. They are not necessarily activated except in people working on themselves and making successful connections to higher states of being, or sometimes by accident, for example as a result of shock. In this case their impact can be too much for the individual consciousness to withstand. These latter four circuits are, at least metaphorically, interstellar by nature. Whereas Circuits 1 to 4 are earthbound, and therefore under the influence of gravity, Circuits 5 to 8 are not so restricted and exist in a realm akin to zero gravity. Some psychedelic drugs offer access to these 'outer' circuits, and it is interesting to note that terms such as 'spacing out' which are used to describe the experience, aptly convey the effect on the unprepared psyche of opening these circuits.

The major protagonists in the 'Star Trek' TV series relate quite well to the first four circuits. Circuit 1 equates with Scotty (the physically involved engineer), Circuit 2 to Dr McCoy (the emotionally involved medic), Circuit 3 to Mr Spock (the intelligence agent, first officer) and Circuit 4 to Captain Kirk (the controller or captain of the ship, the 'terrestrial' decision-maker who holds the ship together). The four remaining circuits then represent the intelligences from 'outer space' that they meet and interact with on their travels. While this might not be the most perfect analogy it holds up in an interesting way. It can also help you to start looking for the manifestation of these circuits in other experiences in life, both those from your personal life but also, for instance, in other art forms. The works of surrealism, for example, offer very exciting and interesting possibilities in this way.

CIRCUIT 1: THE SURVIVAL SYSTEM

This is the basic survival system which is primarily involved with bio-survival. It sets up either/or situations based on advance or retreat. You either advance towards nourishing, protective things or you retreat from threatening things. It sets up walls of timidity, anxiety, and dependence, to a lesser

The Eight Circuits or Systems

A Circuits 1–4:

	BRAIN	left lobe/terrestrial survival		
SYSTEM	1	2	3	4
NAME	survival	territorial	semantic	domestic
ALTERNATIVE NAMES	oral/root	anal/ emotional	manual/ symbolic	moral/ sexual
INPUT FUNCTION	newborn individual	toddler/ trickster	learning child	adolescent [group]
INTEGRATIVE FUNCTION	demanding infant	fighting child	skilful child	parent [culture]
OUTPUT FUNCTION	parent bonding	political child	creative child	actualising individual
LIFE TYPE	unicellular	vertebral	hominid	civilised
LIFE EXPERIENCE	biosurvival	emotional/ ego politics	student/ searcher	centralised domesticity
BASIC IMPRINT	mothering/ nurture	toddling/ nature	symbolic/ artefacts	puberty/ mating
TIME AND SPACE EXPERIENCE	no time experience/ one dimension	experience of time/ two dimensions	concept of time/ three dimensions	conscious of time/ four dimensions

B Circuits 5–8:

	BRAIN	right lobe/future evolution		
SYSTEM	5	6	7	8
NAME	holistic	collective	genetic	atomic
ALTERNATIVE NAMES	neuro-somatic	neuro-electric	meta-programming	meta-physiological
INPUT FUNCTION	hedonic/meditation	ESP/power	DNA awareness	cosmic awareness
INTEGRATIVE FUNCTION	hedonic/yoga	neuro-logic/shaman	DNA alchemy	cosmic powers
OUTPUT FUNCTION	hedonic tantra	collective conscious-ness	DNA fusion/symbiosis	cosmic fusion
LIFE TYPE	freefall	connec-tions	immortality	union
LIFE EXPERIENCE	somatic rapture	neuro-electric	neuro-genetic	satori/samadhi
BASIC IMPRINT	ecstatic experience	bio-chemical dissonance	yogic/mystic	death/OOBE/shock/magick
TIME AND SPACE EXPERIENCE	non-linear modes/the soul dimension	synchron-icities/archetypal dimensions	limitless and open/the total universe	totality exists/endless multiverses

or greater degree. The way through these walls is learning confidence in oneself, especially self-confidence, independence and the willingness to explore what appear to be 'dangerous' pathways. A famous actor once said: 'You are either dangerous or dead'. This could be the watchword of this circuit.

People who have built strong walls based upon this circuit tend to be fat rather than thin, narcissistic about their appearance and to exhibit body symptoms whenever anything 'goes wrong'.

This system is set up during parental bonding, particularly that with the mother who teaches the child a kind of passivity in the face of bio-survival issues. This system, called by Gurdjieff 'the movement centre', evolved on the planet with unicellular life maybe four million or so years ago, as the reptilian brain.

CIRCUIT 2: THE TERRITORIAL SYSTEM

This is the circuit of territory and emotional reaction. It is involved with 'ego politics', the ego status within the pack, and it is here that the simplest pack-bonding functions are instigated. The individual's relationship with this circuit is programmed at the toddler stage. Walls of submission and doubt are built through distortions here, which can most effectively be overcome through learning how to be self-confident and dominant (in appropriate ways and appropriate situations). You are either top dog or underdog, both in social situations and how you view yourself internally. So long as this circuit is distorted, we can say, along with the gestalt therapists, that the underdog always wins. The key is to learn to separate from both top dog and underdog and then choose whichever is appropriate. This is often the dominant 'top dog', once its distortions are seen through and corrected.

People who are primarily acting from this circuit tend to be thin rather than fat types and emotional in their primary interaction with the world. They work from what they call their 'feelings', which are usually no more than basic, reactive emotions. To varying degrees of consciousness, they see the world as a place for giving or taking orders. The classic 'trickster' is found here.

This circuit, called by Gurdjieff 'the false emotional centre', originated with the first mammals maybe 500 million years ago and is closely associated with vertebral life.

CIRCUIT 3: THE SEMANTIC SYSTEM

This is the circuit of language, semantics and symbols. The concepts of time and three dimensional space are born with this circuit. It is concerned with manual as well as laryngeal skills, and is the circuit of analysis, reasoning and labelling the world. The basic programming of this circuit takes place during the child's chief learning periods, both at home and at school.

This circuit is concerned with dividing things (analysis) or connecting them (horizontal synthesis). Distortions to this system set up walls of inarticulate or clumsy communication and dexterity, and the distorted functioning of this system will lead the person so affected to have (or imagine they have) a dumb mind. These walls can be overcome through the learning of skills, both in speech and symbolic communication and in physical dexterity. You can become fluent and be seen (both by yourself and others) as having a good, intelligent, even wise mental set.

People typically working from this circuit tend to be rational types, sometimes termed cerebrotonic. The almost archetypal, very advanced alien with a thin wizened body and a large, overdeveloped cranium is a spoof on this circuit.

Called by Gurdjieff 'the false intellectual centre', this circuit originated with the appearance of humans maybe around 100,000 years ago, and is typical of the early human societal ages such as the Neolithic and Bronze Age where languages were developing along with skills in tool making.

CIRCUIT 4: THE DOMESTIC SYSTEM

This, the domestic or moral circuit, is primarily involved with the socio-sexual aspects of our lives, and is typified by the development of centralised social systems – whether called socialism or capitalism. Patriarchal civilisation (as we know it today) is the apotheosis of an overbearing distortion of this system. It is a function of adolescence, both in terms of the individual, but also in terms of societies and the human race as a whole.

Distortions to this circuit are more complex than with the earlier three. Walls can be set up of either aspect of its primary duality. There are, thus, walls of obedience and walls of disobedience, of morality and immorality (and the attendant guilt). It is in essence the primary circuit of social or tribal conditioning. It is basically imprinted on the genital energy level at the onset of adolescence, but is, of course, well set up and rooted in earlier imprinting and conditioning both from the parents and the society in general. The typical walls of this circuit are generally hard to overcome, and require much work involving de-conditioning and re-imprinting on the genital and sexual levels.

Typical of this circuit are both the 'normally functioning', sexually moral human being and the sexual 'society-level outlaw'. Both are still living within the conditioned walls here.

Go too far and the society will either pull you back or put you away. The highest distortions of this circuit are seen in the more extreme moralist figures of our society (walls of tightness and holding), or in the rapists and sexual manipulators (walls of over-looseness and moral diarrhoea) who appear to be becoming more rife as the basic imprinting levels of this circuit are breaking down with the onset of the New Age.

Circuit 4 developed in tandem with the development of urbanised civilisation, and is the circuit of cities and the modern western world. It brings cancer and heart disease when it operates in a distorted way. Gurdjieff called it 'the false personality'. It is said to be developmentally connected to the neo-cortex, originating maybe 30,000 years ago.

CIRCUIT 5: THE HOLISTIC SYSTEM

This circuit, the holistic, is the one most recently activated in human consciousness and can be seen manifesting and developing in the New Age movement. Its primary functions are involved with ecstatic experiences and what has been termed 'hedonic engineering'. It is about the freedom and right of both the individual and societies to make their own decisions about what to put into themselves – physically, emotionally, mentally, spiritually, or in any other way – and what to leave out, to refuse to take on board. It is intimately connected with the growth of the soul, both the individual and the group soul. Its clear manifestation leads to synergy, neurosomatic rapture, clear self-identification and the ability to effectively dis-attach from the contents of the personality. Its distortions appear in walls of attachment and hedonistic immaturity and addiction.

The holistic circuit is global and pantheistic in orientation, it is inclusive of wholes wherever possible. Gurdjieff called it 'the magnetic centre'. It is said to have evolved with the right brain maybe only 4000 years ago. People who function from this place are highly creative, artistically or scientifically, and typify the image of 'the agony and the ecstasy'. They tend to be Jung's intuitive types, and seen as the directors of their lives. They are self-actualising. Their goal is the transcendence of global restrictions and, it is said, ultimately space migration. It has been suggested this circuit is preparing us for just that.

CIRCUIT 6: THE COLLECTIVE SYSTEM

This is the circuit of collective consciousness, of making connections in a magical or shamanic fashion, and of the appearance of synchronicities. It accesses archetypal dimensions. Turning on this circuit necessitates the joining of the conscious circle of humanity, being connected to the totality of human consciousness. Gurdjieff called it 'the true emotional centre' and it is said to have evolved around 2500 years ago with the full evolution of the right neo-cortex.

This circuit is the source of archetypal dreams, and when functioning at least effectively if not fully, lets the participant access the very blueprints of life, sometimes called the akashic records or the DNA archives. It has two typical deities in Pan and Gaia.

The ability to abstract clearly is opened up here, and the functioning of this circuit leads to a geometrical increase in intelligence. It also opens up the possibilities of ESP, telepathy, and communication with higher intelligences.

CIRCUIT 7: THE GENETIC SYSTEM

This circuit is that of DNA awareness and fusion, neurogenetic bliss and even immortality. It is the circuit of the gnostic soul. Whereas Circuit 6 involved the collective consciousness of humanity, this one involves the collective consciousness of all life. Gurdjieff called it 'the true intellectual centre', and it is said to be evolving right now with the development of new brain patterns and connections. Its functioning offers the possibility of complete self-programming, the full consciousness of consciousness. It links the participant to the divine dance, and opens up the possibility of conscious reincarnation, past life memories, and interspecial symbiosis.

CIRCUIT 8: THE ATOMIC SYSTEM

The atomic system is concerned with full cosmic awareness and ultimately cosmic fusion. It is the circuit of samadhi, union with the highest or deepest self or god. It is no longer a circuit of the universe as it holds and transcends all multiverses. Gurdjieff called it 'the essence'. It can be touched on by highly evolved individuals but has not developed to any noticeable degree in the circle of humanity. Concerned with cosmic engineering, it is non-local in its manifestation and total at one and the same time. Anything said about it is a contradiction for it incorporates all duality. Its full development can lead to the transcendence of the space–time continuum.

The Tree of Life

The Tree of Life is the map of the guidebook that is known as the Qabalah. For a full description of this map, and how to use it in many practical ways, see my book *The Living Qabalah*.

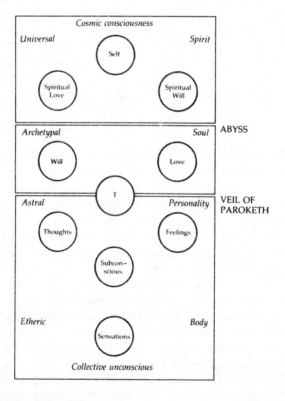

Figure 2: The Tree of Life

The Qabalah is a constant inspiration to seekers after inner wisdom, whatever their religion or belief. While being a seemingly endless source of spiritual insight and experience, the Qabalah also emphasises the relevance of our ordinary, daily lives as an expression of our spirituality. The Qabalah offers us a detailed, coherent world view, both of the nature of human existence and the relationship between ourselves, other beings, our planet and even the universe as a whole.

The word Qabalah means 'to reveal', and it refers to the revelation of your own inner nature that can come from its study and use. There are many different ways to describe the Tree of Life, and an equally large number of ways of using it. This Tree is a guide to the territory of life, including the personality, the soul and the spirit. It encompasses a philosophy and psychology of great theoretical and practical depth that deals with the whole person, not just the intellect, and it has been called 'the Mysticism of the West'.

Being both easy to visualise and memorise, the Tree of Life serves as a useful and potent guide to the individual human being. It helps you to be exactly who you are right at this moment, and to understand more fully where you have come from and where you wish to go to. It is also relevant, through the growth of the individual, to the evolution of the whole planet. By understanding and acting upon the central theme of the Qabalah, that we must recognise and own everything that we are, we not only grow for ourselves but we come to a greater understanding of the workings of our universe as well.

Julia's story is a good example of how using the Tree can aid personal growth. Working as an art teacher, she felt her work in no way satisfied her inner desires to be a 'true artist'. Through studying the Tree of Life, she was able to clarify the different areas of her experience, and enhance her positive qualities without in any way suppressing her darker side. She gained a clearer understanding of her inner polarities, her anima and animus, and was able to apply this new knowledge to her daily experience. She still works as a teacher, but now uses this work to express her creativity and to share her excitement and connection to art with others.

The Tree of Life is composed of eleven spheres. At the root end of the Tree is the sphere called Malkuth, which represents the body, the physical world and the connection between these two, the senses. At the top of the Tree is Kether, which represents the most central, or deepest aspect of our spiritual being, the place where our individuality blurs into union with all other consciousness. The spheres between these two, and the complex array of paths that connect them, represent all the other aspects of our being. As we learn to have practical experience of these different spheres so we add to our knowledge of the different parts of ourselves.

Mike usually had his head in the clouds. He did not really want to be here, and at any excuse would enter into situations and experiences that kept him disconnected and safe from the 'gross heaviness of everyday life'. His only real interest was music. As his work with the Tree of Life progressed, he started meditating on the lower parts of the Tree, those parts that relate to our personality and everyday existence. He found it exciting to visualise Malkuth, and really feel his physical presence on the earth. While still no pragmatic businessman, Mike now runs his own small studio and helps other young people get a start in the music business.

The Tree of Life offers a way of clarifying what is inside you, and helps you express this understanding, whether in the actions and events of everyday life, or through symbols, myths or dreams. You are more able to relate who you are, and what you do, to other people, however apparently different or diverse from yourself. My god may not have the same name as yours, but our communication is greatly enhanced when we discover the common ground of our experience.

The spheres on the Tree of Life also correspond to the human body. Through experiencing these spheres, we can come to a greater understanding of our body energies and the relationship within us between physical, emotional and mental charges. This has great importance therapeutically, and many people who work with others as helpers, whether as direct body workers, or as psychotherapists, find the Qabalistic map most useful.

Many methods of personal development and spiritual growth attest to the essential identity between what is inside (the microcosm) and what is outside (the macrocosm). In the middle of the Tree is a sphere called Tiphareth which represents both the sun (at the centre of the solar system) and the heart (at the centre of the human system). Through meditation, visualisation and other Qabalistic exercises, we can make a practical connection between our inner life and the world outside. The ultimate goal of the Qabalah is the full, living realisation of this connection. This not only aids in the development of individual harmony but also furthers the cause of international and planetary peace.

The Tree of Life has been described as the living temple of the spirit. It is the individual and the universe as expressed through that individual. In the light of the Qabalah, as seen through the Tree of Life, the shadows of all transient things are instantly banished. The answers to the great questions: Who am I? Why am I here? What can I do next? How can I be myself? and so on are clearly given to the diligent user of this map.

Overlaying The Maps

It is generally not a good idea to overlay different maps. While there are obvious similarities and this can be done, it can lead to confusion, and lessens the impact of each of the individual maps themselves. It is far better to learn different maps – particularly the three described above – and to practise holding them all in awareness, then using each as seems appropriate to any situation. It is possible to overlay these maps, however, and it can be useful so long as the resulting correspondences are not treated too seriously.

Seeking a Guide

It is said that the path of true transformation concentrates on attending to various needs as they come into consciousness. These needs may require transformation and change or they may simply require action and fulfilment. Whatever is the case, however, a time occurs in the individual's development when it is appropriate to seek the help of another person – a guide. As said at the beginning of this chapter, the guide needs to be experienced and willing, and may be a friend, a therapist, a guru or whatever. They must always be seen for what they are, however, as aids along the way, helping the traveller in one part of his or her journey. Then a session with a guide can be seen as a little microcosm of the greater journey of life. Or it may be simply a segment of life itself, focused on and developed in a way that enhances the future manifestation of the individual traveller. In either case it will be effective if it enhances the journey and ineffective if it does not.

All individual sessions with a guide, in whatever form they may take, can be seen as having three basic parts: the purpose, the intention and the plan.

PURPOSE

The soul energises parts of the personality that have the potential to manifest the individual more fully in some way. The soul grows in this way, learning the lessons for which it chose to incarnate in the first place. Looking at problems and issues that arise in this way brings the realisation that these issues are never isolated from the soul. As the process continues, the soul and the individual move gradually closer.

The good guide sees nothing 'right' or 'wrong' about the manifestation of this process, but simply acknowledges the soul and assists in moving the individual in the required direction. He or she will also help the traveller find the next step for the manifestation of potential. The guide and the traveller both have to learn to trust and stay with the process.

Relax and centre

Think of a difficulty you are experiencing or have recently experienced in your life. Allow yourself to picture the situation(s) involved, to hear any words that may connect with what is happening, and to feel all the associated feelings.

Now think of any other similar difficulties you currently have or have had in the recent past. Again allow real situations to emerge into your consciousness. Allow the memories to unfold. You may want to write down ideas and images as they occur to you.

Now connect these memories and see if you can find connections and common patterns between your current or recent difficulties. Look for themes that throw light on the connections. Ask yourself: what is the underlying purpose here? Why is this happening? What is the soul wanting to happen next?

Be aware that all these different aspects are manifestations of the same principles within you, those of love and will. You will learn more of these 'archetypes' as your study of this book progresses.

INTENTION

Initially you are motivated by your wants and needs. By paying attention to these needs, and connecting to their purpose, you can clearly connect with your intention. What do you really need to happen here? How active is your will? What is blocking your expression of this need? Who is aware?

A good guide will expand the choices available to a traveller, make him or her more of a free agent, able to make appropriate choices. The guide will evoke the traveller's true will, their personal power, and also attend to clarifying their connection to love and awareness. The guide will help the client make their centre of consciousness, their 'I', into a 'true home' and encourage them to spend more time there. They will focus on the emergence of archetypes.

It is important to expand problems until they connect to a greater whole. This may be achieved through simple procedures and techniques such as stating the obvious, making the implicit explicit, giving personal responses (but not judgements) and allowing insights and intuitions space to emerge (and not worrying if they are off mark). Of primary importance is making the negative become positive, a move from motivational responses ('I do not want something') to intentional statements ('I want something'). This leads to a real qualitative change, moving the focus from the personality to the soul.

THE PLAN

Whatever happens in a session between two people, it is of vital importance to ground or manifest the realisations, so they do not remain unrooted and unmanifest. We will be dealing in depth with grounding in a later chapter. For now just note the importance of grounding and of manifesting the next step in your progress.

A good guide should be understanding and accepting and at the same time directing and supporting change. He or she must play the role of both a mother and a father to the traveller. As a mother the guide will be with the client, go with the flow, will not interfere and will be gentle. As a father he or she will be surprising, not offering too much security, nudging and stretching the traveller whenever and however possible. It is important for the guide to remember to offer both functions. Then the guide will function as an effective external unifying centre whose constant aim is to put back this centre into the client's own consciousness or sphere of awareness.

A guide needs to encourage resolution of patterns that are held from, say, the traveller's relationship with his mother or father, and not allow the unclear projection of these attributes. He or she needs to change dependence into autonomy, although for a while it may be appropriate to build and allow dependence to manifest. You have to allow and accept before you can effectively change and develop. Both participants in any relationship should honour each other and be thankful for the opportunity of being together. Roberto Assagioli said: 'Gratefulness is what opens the channels between us in higher realms'. In many ways the most important question in any session is: what is happening between you and me right now?

The 'Inner Guide'

We all have a source of wisdom and understanding that knows who we are, where we have been and where we are going. Our own 'inner guide' is in tune with our unfolding Purpose or True Will and clearly senses the next step to be taken in the unfoldment of this purpose. As we contact it we can better recognise the difficulties we are having in our growth and, with its help, can guide our awareness and will towards the resolution of these difficulties. Rightly used it can help us direct our energies towards achieving integration in our personality, and towards unifying the personality, soul and spirit into one living reality.

Many images are associated with this source of inner guidance, including the Guardian Angel, the sun, a diamond, a fountain, a star, an eagle, a dove, a phoenix, Christ, Buddha, a Wise Old Man or Woman. Different images emerge to meet different needs, and according to the development, culture and conditioning of the individual. In general terms it is often found that a 'masculine' image is encouraging, stimulating and inspiring while a 'feminine' image is nurturing, supportive and allowing. This is not always the case, however. Whatever image you choose (or chooses you) it is an easy matter to contact this inner guide.

There are many complicated rituals and procedures for contacting the Guardian Angel or Wise Old Person inside yourself to assist your growth. The following procedure, however, is not only simple but also very effective.

Relax and centre. Take some time to let your body really become comfortable, but remain alert.

Close your eyes, take a few deep breaths and let appear in your imagination the face of a wise old person whose eyes express great love for you.

Engage him/her in dialogue, and, in whatever way seems best use the presence and guidance to help you understand better whatever questions, directions, choices, problems, etc., you are dealing with *at this moment*. This dialogue can be verbal or non-verbal, taking place on a visual and symbolic level of communication and understanding.

Spend as much time as you need with this wise old person, then thank the image for having appeared to you, return to normal consciousness and write down what has happened.

You may not, particularly after some practice, actually need to imagine a person – he or she may be heard as a sort of inner voice, or even a direct 'knowing' what is the best thing for you to be doing in any given situation. This wise old person does not always have to be of the same sex each time he or she appears, or even to have a similar appearance; and remember to check the validity of all messages.

John did this inner dialogue exercise and his 'Guardian Angel' appeared as a young child. 'I always like young children as carriers of wisdom,' he wrote. 'I saw the child as parentless,

I wanted it to be the first child and I knew inside that his name was Adam. He was dressed in white and was blond. . . I say he but really the child was hermaphrodite. The wisdom he communicated to me was connected to a centre somewhere inside, directly, not through words. . . The child was always silent, like a kind of watcher. Wisdom is silence.'

(You can adapt this simple procedure to dialogue with anything else, for example a part of your body. Try this: have an inner dialogue with, say, your left hand and see what it has to tell you. Involve the hand in its external form, but also include its inner form, too – the bones, flesh and blood that all go to make the hand what it is.)

· 4 ·

ONCE UPON A TIME
Exploring Fate

*'Some people say we're born with our fate. Others say we
make our fate with our actions. Witches say it's neither, and
that something else catches us like the dog catcher catches a
dog. The secret is to be there if we want to be caught or not
to be there if we don't.*

FLORINDER DONNA

We can indulge in the past, or we can go there with purpose, to
find out what has happened to us and how the walls around us
have been built up. Through this knowledge we can then find
how to dismantle a wall – or at the very least, take a few blocks
out of it.

Whatever we discover from the past we need to integrate into
our present situation – into our thoughts, our feelings, and most
particularly our bodies, where tensions and armouring hold the
pain, the anxiety, and all the other blocks from the past. It
is a mistake to think because we want spiritual connection,
transpersonal insights, or some kind of inner illumination, that
we can or should transcend our bodies. It is through our bodies
that we can really transform who we are right now. That is the
only thing that is possible for us, because we are here and now
and no where or no time else – right here and now in this reality
we are creating.

Material from the past comes up spontaneously, all the time,
and there is nothing wrong with that, or with just observing
it and letting it go. But when we start working consciously on
ourselves, we find that the stuff that does come up is relevant
to what we are currently working on. For example, Jonathan
remembered that as a baby every time he started walking his
mother would pick him up and praise him for his strength and
cleverness. Of course she meant no harm, you might say she

was being really encouraging, which she undoubtedly was. Yet now Jonathan has problems sustaining things; at the onset, his willpower to do things is very strong, but once he gets started he cannot carry things through.

By remembering his mother picking him up every time he started to walk and, connecting it with his current issue, he realised that in so doing she had inadvertently interfered with his ability to keep going. If she had but let him continue walking until he reached his destination, or fall in the process of trying, before picking him up and praising him, the issue of sustaining his intent would not be a problem. The memory, and the subsequent work he did on it, which included some of the exercises you will do in this chapter, helped Jonathan to become more whole through being able to finish things (or make a good attempt at so doing).

One technique Jonathan used was the following exercise, for which you will need four sheets of paper, at least A4 size but the larger the better. You will also need a set of coloured crayons, pencils or pens.

Relax and centre.

Put one sheet of paper in front of you and follow these instructions:

Ask yourself: 'Where do I come from?'

Allow any answers that come up to emerge freely. Don't censor or judge, just be aware of whatever answers you have to this question.

Keep repeating the question to yourself until you feel you have answered it fully.

Close your eyes, and let a picture, image or symbol emerge in your consciousness that answers for you the question: 'Where do I come from?'
When you have such an image, open your eyes and draw it on the paper before you. Use as much or as little colour

as you like, and remember this does not have to be a great work of art. It is a symbolic representation of your answer to the question.

If you wish, you can write any words or ideas you want to record on the back of the drawing.

When it is completed, put it to one side, move a clean piece of paper in front of you, let go of the image you have just drawn, take a couple of deep breaths, and continue with the rest of the exercise.

Repeat the same procedure until you have four drawings, one on each of your four pieces of paper. The questions to answer for the remaining drawings are:

'Where do I want to go?'

'What stops me reaching my destination?'

'What do I need to help me grow?'

When you have completed all four drawings, place them so you can see all four at once and spend some time connecting to the symbols and images you have drawn. See if you can find practical ways to:

- move you closer to where you want to go;
- overcome the resistances that hinder your progress;
- manifest what you need to help you grow.

All our resistances were necessary at some point to help us survive, so it is not appropriate just to tear old walls down. Respect the resistance, and as you get to know it find out what is on the other side of the wall of resistance. Find ways of connecting with this energy, with the quality within it, and you will find the wall will become obsolete. You will not need to tear it down, it will dissolve, having been an illusionary barrier all along. Remember that you need to experience something fully before disattaching from it. You all know by now that just wishing does not make it go away!

When memories of the past arise, do not get caught up in their story, the content, but find how the memory fits into your current, ongoing context. By working on the present context of the past pattern, you can learn to control and transform it in a regulatory rather than a restrictive way. You can change from being a victim of past circumstances and events to being in charge of your life.

It is most appropriate to delve into the past when:

- a particular behaviour, experience or pattern is inconsistent with the rest of your personality, and it will not integrate with the whole.

  For example, we all know people who are fairly competent on the whole but who have one area in their life which is a complete mess; perhaps it is to do with their relationship to members of the opposite sex, or their ability, like Jonathan mentioned above, to sustain their effort until they get what they want.

- when a part of you acts (or more probably re-acts) in an inappropriate way that is out of proportion to the event involved.

  For example, some people, even when they have more than enough money, do not let go of their fear about not having enough!

- where you have habits and phobias, especially ones around fear, shame, or guilt.

  For example, is there something you think you ought to give up (whether you actually need to or not)?

- when you undertake persistent self-destructive behaviour, sabotaging your progress.

  For example, there are people who just cannot get through an interview. They may be bright, self-motivated people with pleasant personalities, but when confronted with an interview they come across as bland, characterless nonentities.

Before continuing, think of ways that you fit into these four groups or types.

Relax and centre.

Connect with a memory from your past, any memory at all. Let it emerge from your unconscious. Take note of any images, sounds or feelings associated with this memory. Allow yourself to experience it fully right now.

Pay particular attention to how you feel in your body when this memory is being experienced. Take some time to connect with this, then exaggerate your body posture, sensations and (if appropriate) movements so that you experience even more.

Now get an image that represents this memory. Remember that images and symbols are the language of the unconscious. Do not censor or judge the image, just let it emerge.

Pay attention to this image, look for details within it; do not just focus on its central theme, look around the edges too.

Now change the image in any way that seems appropriate to you. Let your imagination run free and consciously change the image until it becomes less threatening, more pleasing, totally different, whatever. You are in control of this image, it is not in control of you.

When you have changed the image, imagine it large and bright in front of you, then draw its energy into your body. Really feel this new, positive energy filling you with its life-enhancing qualities.

Mary's image, associated with the time her father left home, was of the house she had lived in then being on fire. She saw this clearly, felt the heat of the flames, heard the crackling of burning wood, and cried as smoke got in her eyes. She connected with the depression, sadness and anguish associated with that sad time in her life.

She changed the image by imagining a fire engine arriving, and putting out the flames. Then decorators came and made the house into a home again, this time the dream home she had always wanted. When she merged with the new image, she not only felt better in herself, she also realised how her sadness over her father's departure had stopped her taking pride in her own house where she lives now. She also realised that both her mother and she had been happier after he had left!

Patterns from the past create dreams, images, memories, ways of relating, ways of using our bodies, daydreams and so on. All these ways of imaging, and any associated pattern from the past, can be reconstructed or reframed. In esoteric lore it is said that a pattern caused your birth. In other words you come into your earthly existence with patterns already formed. They are what your soul has chosen to work on throughout this life. So in this sense your soul, who you really are, chose the birth you had, and that experience was your primary way of setting up what you would be like, how you would interrelate with the world, and what walls you would have for this life.

Try to share any new learning or understanding from these previous exercises with someone else, someone you know well and trust. To do this will help you ground the experiences, and make them more real.

Childhood Development

A lot happens in an individual's development through childhood. We are only dealing here with some of the issues that are most relevant to our current investigation. As you read this section, refer back to the Eight Circuits map of consciousness and see how the information here fits into that model of experience.

From birth until about two years of age is a time, primarily, for connecting to the basic archetypes of existence. These include the experience of birth itself, the meaning and purpose of incarnation, 'having a new start', and so on. The actual experiences undergone during this period form walls around these archetypal energies which will persist through life. For instance, how you view and relate to your purpose for being here, and how you deal with new beginnings in your life will be set up at this time.

Most early relating, certainly that of greatest significance, is with your parents. On this primary level you learn how much you can trust (or mistrust) the world around you. During this 'oral phase', which is basically about survival, you learn ways of dealing with the question: Am I going to make it? During this period there are many ways that walls can be set up. If you learn that you cannot trust your environment you might decide to attempt to control it instead. You could become, at least partially, the sort of person who needs to be in control, who is manipulative of other people.

Between the ages of two and four, or thereabouts, the focus changes on to issues of self-confidence and autonomy, and how you deal (or do not deal) with these issues. Such energies can become distorted into shame and a sense of worthlessness. During this stage of life, which has been termed 'the anal phase', the primary archetypal energies you deal with are self-control, assertion, independence, and having boundaries. Should you confirm or should you assert yourself? How can you give and take love? How can you assert yourself? Should you control yourself in this situation? You are learning to live a life that is separate from your parental base. Walls that may get set up here will be concerned with lack of a true sense of individuality and self, self-depreciation and shame. Along with many other children in our controlling society, you may learn to say to yourself, in one way or another: 'I am not powerful so I don't feel good'. Such a state can lead to the withholding of feelings, opinions, and free expression. 'If you really saw what I'm like inside, you wouldn't love me anymore.'

In her relationship with her mother, Lin threw away the positive, good things along with the bad, negative things. When she worked on this issue, she realised her mother's positive qualities included the ability to excite, generosity and optimism. But her mother held her back. In a session where she imagined dialoguing with her mother she said most clearly: 'You held me down, you wanted me to be what you wanted'. Lin 'mothered' her boyfriend in the same way she had been mothered. She projected on to him just what her mother did to her. She learned that she needs to assert herself but not to mother or nag him. 'I want to be me, not my mother.'

Yet what could her mother actually do to her now? Asked this very question, Lin became very small, like a frightened child, and memories came up of how her mother would humiliate her in front of other children and adults. She felt very vulnerable. What she needed was care, comfort and warmth. If she could get that now, perhaps through giving those very qualities to herself in a way her mother could not, she realised she could change the pattern. By caring for herself more, and remembering not to project on to her boyfriend, Lin found she could express herself more clearly.

Between the ages of approximately four and six years, the primary archetype being made manifest in the child is initiative. Its distortion manifests as guilt, or fear of unity. Sometimes called 'the phallic phase', this time of life is connected to the emerging sexual drive. This new energy is 'lived out', as it were, with the parents (particularly the one of the opposite sex). The child of this age tends to identify with the parent of the same sex and challenge the other parent. Male and female polarities and identity come into play. Often there is a desire for 're-union' with the earlier phases, even with the spiritual realm. 'I'm afraid of being here again, living another life of pain and hardship.'

Between the ages of (approximately) six until the onset of puberty, we enter what has been called the 'latency' period. This is not really the most appropriate name for a period when the child is learning how to operate in the world which he or she has now set up. It is a time of great exploration. The primary archetypes operating here are exploration and worthiness. The person learns to judge themselves as worthy or unworthy. For many reasons, parents often do not support the growth of independence and exploration during this period. Perhaps they cannot let go of their own fears and worthlessness. The mother may become (unconsciously) seductive, wanting to keep the child as a child. The father may become threatening and repressive for similar reasons. A good external model can be most useful, to help the child find connection with the relevant archetypes. A lack of connection and clarity at this stage can set up walls of inferiority and unworthiness. The child might not want to be incarnated, or might set up the situation where he or she will become a perfectionist in later life, always to meet unreal and inflated goals.

Sandy was a very gifted child, very intelligent and self-expressive. He found himself in a doubly threatening situation. The other children in his class at school could not accept him (or he viewed it that way) and his father did not support his explorations. He felt threatened to his very core and realised he had to find a way of protecting himself from this aggression. He started stuttering! This stutter persisted in later life, and only by learning to accept himself, then talking about himself and his wishes in a relaxed centred way was he able to overcome it – and then only partially.

When puberty comes, along with the onset of adolescence, the main issues are those of identity and role, both as an individual and as a social being. Genital sexuality also emerges as a primary concern. The child's body goes through the well-known changes and these herald the end of childhood in a physical sense. Depending upon the level of success in dealing with the issues that have gone before, however, childhood in an emotional or intellectual sense may be far from over. Indeed, many people never fully develop beyond this early adolescent stage. They may lead (apparently) effective lives, but inwardly they are a mess of unresolved crises and ill-formed archetypal connections. If things do not go well during this period, the person does not get a sense of their true birthright, their innate worthiness as individual sparks of consciousness. Indeed, as developmental crises from the earlier stages of life inevitably reappear, rather than being taken in their stride, they can be re-enacted in ways that lead to much pain and sorrow. It has been suggested that many of the 'worse' aspects of adolescence are the result of just this kind of unresolved re-enactment.

While he may not have actually said as much, John's father's actions, words and feelings towards his son communicated to John that his father thought his son unworthy. At a deep base level, John learned to view himself as worthless – 'my father told me I'm no good, he must be right'. This sense of worthlessness led him to cut off any degree of sustained relating with another person by going into a diffuse, unformed emotional state he termed 'being a spludge'.

During some deep bodywork, John made a connection with his heart, and said it felt like there was an empty hole there.

Within this dark hole he visualised a standing stone, situated on a bleak, windswept moor. It was dark and it rained continuously. He touched the stone and acknowledged its presence in his heart and this was the beginning of a real transformation for him. He was not ready to transform the image (and thus his connection with his heart), but through acknowledging its presence he had made the first, and most vital step. At the end of the session, John said he wanted 'a freedom that accepts time and place'. During the weeks that followed he returned to the moor several times, he meditated on the image of the stone, and he did a large painting of it. Over time his body became a bit looser, and he started to feel heart connections emerging that he had never felt before. He took in a stray kitten and nurtured it back to health, and in so doing nurtured his own inner heart connection.

Such work is a long, ongoing process, but unless, like John, we are willing to step forward and at least acknowledge our inner pain, we can never move towards transformation.

Fate Versus Free Will

How many times have you heard a discussion that centres around the issues of fate versus free will? On the one hand, 'fate' can be seen as leading us through the unfoldment of some pre-set pattern. Ultimately, from this position, whatever we do is done because that is our fate. We really have no choice, certainly concerning major life issues. On the other hand, the 'free will' position says we choose everything we do and if there is such a thing as fate it is only something we create through our actions. From this position, whatever we do we have chosen and we have to take the consequences.

The 'fate versus free will' issue is a favourite topic with armchair philosophers. It can often be an avoidance of what our experience tells us. If you think about this in terms of your own life, it is easy to see that there is no 'battle' between these two states. We have both fate and free will. You have the choice, and always have had, to do what you wish with your life (within the bounds you impose upon yourself). In other words your life is not pre-destined and you have freedom to do with it what you will. And, at the very same time, life moves on whether you act or not. Our lives are, therefore, quite simply not ruled by either fate or free will. Like all such illusions of duality, it is always the unfoldment of both that brings us to a closer connection to who we really are.

Your individual connection to both fate and free will is in part genetic, in part environmentally set up, and in part what you bring with you as a soul choosing to incarnate. Yet even this distinction is illusionary, for all three of these are so intimately interwoven to view one as having more influence than another is a mistake. Ultimately it does not matter how you look at it, or what you believe, your life will unfold as it is meant to and, at the very same time, as you want it to. These two apparently contradictory states are, when viewed from the level of the soul, one and the same.

Self-Programming

We are all conditioned, imprinted and programmed. The work of 'walking through walls' or any other method for self-development is to change our connections to the conditioning and imprinting we have previously undergone, and to learn to re-program ourselves in whatever way we choose.

If you compare a human being to a computer, you could say that the imprinting is equivalent to the operating system, the conditioning to memory-resident programs, and the programming to the software we are currently running. Imprinting is partly genetic, partly done in the pre-birth (womb) environment, and partly achieved through very early, pre-conceptual experiences. If we want to change our imprints we have to accept they are so deeply rooted within us we will only achieve meaningful and permanent changes through long, hard work, that might include much pain, shock and difficulty. To change our conditioning is not so difficult, but is still a long, hard process. Conditioning includes all the stuff we 'take on board' from parents, teachers, and the other 'well-meaning' (or otherwise!) people we meet in our formative years. If you think of the Eight Circuits model or the Tree of Life, you can see how different circuits or spheres are conditioned 'as appropriate' to the setting in which we find ourselves. This conditioning is mostly finished by the onset of the teenage years, but is constantly being affected and altered – for example, through political conditioning, advertising and so on. Many of the aims of different schools of therapy, meditation and yoga are concerned with making changes to the negative aspects of our basic conditioning. This is also the aim, of course, of most political 'consciousness-raising' groups, whether the aim is to change the person's basic conditioning around racism, sexism or any other life-restricting pattern.

In its effect, there is little difference between conditioning and programming. Yet, just like with the computer analogy, one is more permanently resident than the other. Your memory-resident programs take more work to change than the software you are running. You can quite easily choose which program to run at any time. Often we do not make such conscious choices, but to make such choosing conscious and active should be a major aim of your growth work. After all, whatever you may have been led to believe, you are the programmer. It is your computer, and you can choose what you wish to do with it.

Even on the level of our deepest imprinting, it is possible that you may have already chosen everything that happens to you in your life even before you were born!

Duality

Everything we experience in life is, in one sense or another, an experience of duality. On a physical level we are either up or down, in or out, left or right, or somewhere in between. On an emotional level we are happy or sad, truthful or dishonest, glad or sad, awake or asleep, and so on.

It has been said that we are 'divided for the chance of union'. This seems a very healthy way of living within our total illusion of duality, for it gives meaning to our experience. You experience duality, you live in a world of opposites, so you have the opportunity of experiencing both poles of the duality, thus increasing your awareness and knowledge, and bringing the poles together so you can experience the ecstasy of reconnection. You come from unity into duality in order to gain experience. When you return once more to unity, you will be as equally one as you were at the outset of your soul journey, and yet you will have been enriched with the experiences you will have had along the way.

The walls we build around ourselves are usually an expression of a connection to a negative or distorted pole of a primary duality. For example, the quality of self-confidence may become a wall of anxiety and fear. Think about the following list of dualities, and try to be aware of some of these walls as you experience them.

dependence	independence
dominance	submission
confidence	doubt
fluency	inarticulateness
dexterity	clumsiness
morality	immorality
conforming	rebellion

Be aware how walls can be erected from either pole of a duality. Are you encumbered by a wall of morality or by a wall of immorality? Would it not be better to have both available to you, then choose which seems appropriate to your situation? Maybe it is never appropriate to be immoral, but at least you will have that option, and your morality will then be self chosen rather than imposed.

Two primary dualities, set up in our early years and clearly described in the first two systems of the Eight Circuits map, are Dominance–Submission and Advance–Retreat.

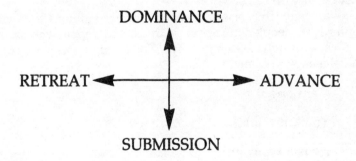

Each pole in these dualities has a clear message:

Dominance:	I'm in charge.
Submission:	You're the boss.

Advance:	I will
Retreat:	I won't

Life is never that simple, however, and we usually exhibit combinations of these four conditions; for example, we might be dominant and yet retreating, or advancing with submission. The use in transactional analysis of descriptions based on whether you feel 'okay' or 'not okay' can help us to understand the resultant messages.

Dominance/Advance:	I'm okay, you're okay
Dominance/Retreat:	I'm okay, you're not okay
Submission/Advance:	I'm not okay, you're okay
Submission/Retreat:	I'm not okay, you're not okay

Which of these four basic modalities do you tend to operate from? What do you need to do in order to change your modality to that of 'dominance and advance' where you see both yourself and your world as okay?

We often have biased ideas on such conditions and view ourselves, people who are close to us, and people who are not so close in quite different ways. For example, with regard to intelligence, you might say:

'I am bright,

You know a lot,

He is a know-all!'

Memories

We go through death and life, death and life, only because that's pulsation, not because it's ending and beginning; there is no such thing.

CHRIS GRISCOM

It is possible to have memories that appear to show that you have lived before, often as a human being on this planet, but sometimes on other planets, in other places, on other planes, and even occasionally as other types of beings. Whatever the 'truth' of such experiences, that is, whether they are 'genuine' memories or not, they can be most relevant and important in your development. It does not really matter whether they are illusionary or not so long as the memory is relevant to you and meaningful in your life. We are not going to enter into a metaphysical discussion about the possibilities of re-incarnation. All that is important is to treat such memories with the level of respect they deserve. If it is meaningful to your life and you can integrate what you learn from such a memory, all well and good. If it merely titillates you, or inflates your ego, you had better watch out!

No one ever experiences a 'genuine' past life that is not relevant to their current growth. When such memories do arise, you can take the opportunity to work on them and to learn what message about yourself they are offering you. It is most interesting to note, also, that when people do start having such memories, they are usually not singular. We remember we have lived many lives before. It is as if we are not merely reincarnations of past selves, but rather that we are on a continuous journey of incarnations – transincarnating over and over until we finally have integrated all the lessons our soul originally came into being to learn.

Blocks to memories of past incarnations may come in many forms, for example simple disbelief that such things are possible, or fear that the memories that may be evoked will be too painful to face, or fear that you will become inflated after realising you were 'Julius Caesar' or some other well-known character from history. These fears are well founded, and such dangers do exist. What seems to be important, however, is not whether the memories are actually 'real' in any way, but whether the memory gives you anything worthwhile to work on in this life right now.

The following exercise will be more effective if you set up an appropriate environment in which to have the experience. You have to choose this for yourself, but perhaps very soft, melodic instrumental music might be useful, candle light, evocative scents, beautiful flowers that are in season, and so on. Really spend some time designing your setting before trying this technique.

Relax and centre.

Take some deep, connected breaths and let yourself drift into a sleep state, but remain alert to what is happening to you. Do not fall asleep!

Think back over this day. What have you done today? Try to recall as much detail as possible, right back to when you woke up this morning.

Now recall yesterday, and again try to remember as much detail as possible. As much as you are able try to think of the evening first, then the afternoon, morning, and finally when you first woke up, but do not get too caught up with the technique, just let it come as naturally as possible.

Now recall last week. What can you remember from the end of last week? And what from the beginning of last week?

What about last month? And last year?

Now recall some striking memories of any kind from ten years or so ago. Allow yourself to remember the experiences, and see what you were like then.

Then recall something from your childhood. What were you like when you were, say, five years old?

Take your time and really relive these memories as fully as possible. When you cannot get much detail, allow your imagination to fill in the 'gaps' in your memory. Trust your ability to choose the right images.

Now allow your consciousness to drift backwards, and simply watch as you enter the spaces and memories that relate to previous lives. Do not censor or judge, just see what images and ideas emerge. It does not matter if they are 'real' or not, because you are choosing right now to connect and whatever emerges will have relevance to you. Do not force it, let memories arise.

Take your time with this. You might not get anywhere the first time you try the exercise, and may need to repeat it several times before memories do occur. In that case, try to do the exercise regularly, and trust there is meaning in what is happening for you.

At the end of each journey into your past, allow yourself to come forward to the present day, here and now in the room from whence you started. Slowly and carefully, stand up, and look around you. Really fix your vision on items in your room. Stamp your feet a few times and perhaps have a drink and something light to eat. It is important you bring your consciousness back to your present reality, regrounding yourself here and now.

Write about your memories in your diary, and use techniques you know already, and those you will learn as your reading of this book progresses, to process any information you have gleaned from your journey. Do not become attached to what you remember, neither fear nor suppress it. 'Good' memories and 'bad' memories have equal relevance to you, and everything you have ever been is part of your progressive path towards full knowledge and understanding of who you are.

'Negative' recurrence is turning the momentary – things that happen here and now and, like all events, pass away – into the momentous – things to which you become identified or attached. It is the making of mountains out of molehills, particularly in the dimensions of time.

'Positive' recurrence, on the other hand, is watching what happens to you as your life progresses, and seeing that the same meanings and purposes can be found in things that happen over and over, even in apparently different forms. Events keep occurring, in different forms perhaps but with the same message, until you are willing to listen and act upon them. Synchronicities, that is co-incidences that appear to make meaningful connections for you, are the most common form of positive recurrence.

We unconsciously re-enact the same events, from past lives or earlier in this life, in an attempt to meet needs that have not yet been met, or learn lessons that have not yet been integrated in our soul's development.

Both the work you might do on your early life experiences (both from childhood and from your womb experiences), and the work of past life recall, can give you the opportunity to discover more about yourself, and manifest your real purpose for being a soul incarnated on this planet at this time. In your workbook start composing your own personal myth. See yourself as a soul who has come into incarnation in this life to learn various lessons and to have various experiences. Treat your life as the unfoldment of a meaningful tale that has purpose and intention in its every twist and turn. Look for the major events and happenings where you either learned a lesson or missed the mark. Both experiences have equal importance in our personal myth. Start writing your myth now. Begin with the customary words: 'Once upon a time. . .' Start living your life, from this moment forwards, as the continuing unfoldment of this exciting and energising story.

· 5 ·

THE DIVISION OF DESIRE
Exploring Process

His 'I' changes as quickly as his thoughts, feelings and moods, and he makes a profound mistake in considering himself always one and the same person; in reality he is always a different person, not the one he was a moment ago.

GEORGE GURDJIEFF

Anything we do, whatever it is, is always a motivated action. We have chosen to do it. It is an expression of a desire which we are now fulfilling. We are not usually aware of it, but desire is what keeps us separate and apart while deluding us, all of the time, that it will bring us together. Desire is a wall of separation that holds the duality of existence in position. We are held within an illusion that we originally created so that we could better relate with and understand the material plane. In order to do this we had to find a way to forget who we are, to be able really to materialise and be here in the world. The way we found was to create desire.

Every action we take is a result of a desire. It is motivated by a longing which, if we could but see it, is always for the same thing – a return to unity. Yet the whole point of being here, incarnated at this time on the planet Earth, is to experience duality, and it is desire itself which gives us such an opportunity. Desire seen this way is both positive and negative, positive in that it helps us to experience the material world, negative in that it deludes us into thinking the material world is the only world. Our task is to walk the fine line between these positive and negative aspects of desire. Then, when appropriate, we can use desire to help us manifest ourselves without delusion. For we then have desire rather than it having us.

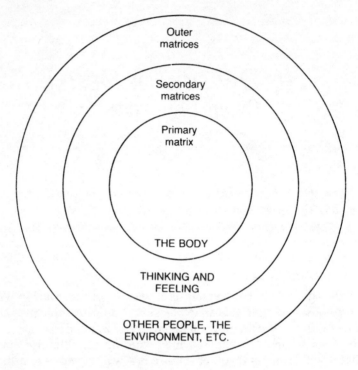

Figure 3: The Matrices of Experience

We sense and feel our desire through various matrices of experience. The body is the primary matrix. It interacts with the world through the senses. This primary matrix is then joined by secondary matrices of desire, namely feelings and thoughts. Third-level matrices are our relationships with other people, either individuals, families, groups of people, countries, species, or the whole of life. When we tune into the third-level matrices, we feel, for example, other people's pain as our own. 'Your pain is my pain.'

As we are constantly interweaving these matrices of desire, we can easily start confusing what we want to do with the messages we get from other matrices: 'what I want is what you want'. Actually what we really want is to merge our uniqueness into a larger matrix. On a deeper, soul level, we are making an attempt to move towards unity. Yet, not being conscious of our own desire, we forget this inner truth, and become 'blobs', as it were, with no connection to our own will.

Other people also impose false connections between matrices. The state decides what is 'right' and what is 'wrong', and parents and teachers, whose matrices are linked closely into the country matrix, help perpetuate this system by teaching their children 'right from wrong'. The people who opt out of this then become disconnected from that matrix. If enough of them disconnect in this way there will be – depending upon the type of state – a change of government, a coup, a revolution, or some other form of change.

To make our own decisions we have to learn how to disattach ourselves from all these third-level matrices so that our decisions are based on our own unique matrices of desire, which, when they are contacted, are found invariably to desire a move towards a true unity based on an active, balanced love. When we contact our true inner matrices of desire, we are connecting with our individual purpose, and, through that, playing a part in the unfoldment of universal Purpose. When you orient these matrices of desire towards the ground, in other words, when you act upon them, you are manifesting more spirit, enlightening the world.

To unify our desire in this way can be a goal which, although we may never actually fully attain it, can give us energy to move towards it, as much as we are able. To do this we have fully to realise that our spiritual or true Purpose is not fixed, for if it was it would block expansion. Our Purpose changes as we change.

Our habits are the primary blocks which compose the wall between us and the attainment of true unification of our desire. This includes physical, emotional and mental habits. Habits lack consciousness and are things we do when we are no more than pre-programmed robots, rather than the free-willed creatures we truly are. Habits are often repeated for a lifetime, as if we fear not to say our prayers at night lest the bogeyman comes and eats us alive. It is our fear of being eaten alive that keeps us from being truly alive!

On the deepest level all desire, including the desire of the Universal Self, is single and complete, and common to all sentient life. Whenever we move towards it, we feel more positive, and whenever we move away from it we feel less positive. The more unity we have in our primary matrix, the body, then within our secondary matrices, the more positive are our feelings and thoughts. Positive feelings and thoughts help create new, better third-level matrices, by removing the conflicts between matrices. Good feelings and thoughts are not the goal in themselves; they are rather the result of our having made conscious choices to move towards desire, then they act as the fuel for our growth and development.

We can most successfully attain these states of positive growth through following the most immediate and true desire as we are experiencing it any moment. True desire is always the one that is accepted and desired not by a majority but by all individual matrices. Otherwise there is conflict. If your physical matrix wants to eat salad, while your mental matrix wants to eat hamburger, for example, you are not connecting to your true desire, for true desire is always harmonious. Your body, your feelings and your mind want the same thing. And when the individual matrices harmonise into a single, true desire, it is found that there is then no conflict with the desires of other people. Harmony is achieved.

Relax and centre.

Think of all the things that you experience *not* as your desire (for example, 'shoulds' – things society makes you do, or that you do for some abstract reason, or habits, or things other people make you do, things you were told you had to do as a child, and so on). Make a list of these things.

Imagine them as blocks in a wall that separates you from being truly yourself.

Imagine taking each of these blocks, one by one, into your hand and as you do so say 'I desire to . . .' whatever it is. So for example, if a block says 'you should brush your teeth every night' then say, as you pick up the block 'I desire to brush my teeth every night'.

Put those blocks that feel right for you to continue using for the present moment on the ground beside you. Those you feel are not appropriate for you to continue using, throw far into the air and watch them disappear in a puff of smoke.

Step forward into the space where the wall was before you changed it, and realise as you do so you are moving towards your true self.

Finally turn around and look at the pile of blocks you choose to keep for the moment. They are appropriate for you to use at this stage of your evolution and incarnation. Say to them: 'I own you and bless you for helping me to manifest.'

Open your eyes, spend some time bringing your consciousness back to your room, then write in your diary about this experience.

When you are stuck within desires, feeling your process is stuck, as it were, then you need to expand your matrices of desire. The main ways of 'releasing the process' like this are through:

- recognising the structure you are in and dis-attaching from it;

- recognising two structures that are in conflict, then holding both to facilitate integration;

- watching the emergence of structures, asking yourself what is going on, and seeing what the spiritual purpose is behind the stuckness. Perhaps it is right to be stuck at this time; if it is not, looking at it this way will help to unstick you;

- recognising dying structures, watching for structures that are in the process of dissolving, then letting go and trusting the process;

- facilitating movement between ground and structure, moving from context to content and vice versa.

Remember that everything you do you want to do. People are not always doing what makes them happiest, but their Purpose unfolds as it is meant to. Trust your inner unfoldment and love your life.

The following exercise helps you to recognise the structures you are in and to learn to watch for the emergence of new structures without conscious interference.

Relax and centre.

Sit comfortably, take a few deep breaths and then close your eyes. Spend some time simply watching what sensations, feelings or thoughts come into your awareness. Do not censor or judge them, or try to change them in any way. Say to yourself: 'I am everything of which I am aware.'

Then open your eyes and, connecting to whatever comes into your awareness first, say: 'I am this'.

Now with eyes still open take in your surroundings: look around you, listen to what you may be able to hear and use your other senses as seems appropriate to you. Then say to yourself: 'I am everything of which I am aware'. Then close your eyes and, connecting to whatever comes into your awareness first, say: 'I am this'.

Like a shattered hologram, each one of us is a part of a whole, original picture, that has become shattered. And like a hologram we still contain, within each minute, little piece of us, the whole picture. So we can find within us all there is to say and do and be. In whatever form you take, whether you are a bird, a mountain, a piece of string, a superbly enlightened living master or a stool – of whatever kind, you are it and it is you. With this potential you can say, and do and be anything, and eventually everything.

The path between where you are now and becoming one with everything, is just as you have chosen it. You make your own length, type and gradient of path; you fill it with all the people and things you need for your journey. Tune in now to where you are on your path, to see yourself just as you are, exactly right at this moment, in perfection: this is you and nothing else but you. At this very moment you are full of your self which is continuous and endless.

You can choose the exact next step for you to take. You always do just that. Now you can do it consciously, stepping forward without a care or a concern, yet with direction and choice, for you have chosen. Remember this right now and act upon your choice. It is your total free will that chose, and as your total free will is completely visible and totally understandable to you, when you are being right who you are at this very moment you can step forward with confidence and joy. You are free to say what you will, to do what you will, to be what you will. You will say and do and be exactly what you need to say, need to do and choose to be. Let go! You are yourself completely when you so choose. Without needing to think about it, or deliberate upon it, or ponder over it, or reinforce it, or decide upon it, or wonder if you should – choose to say or be or do whatever it is you want, right at this very moment, to say, be or do.

The Divided Self

Walls of division keep us separate and divided. We have all heard the phrase 'united we stand, divided we fall'. It is true of the individual who can be divided or united, any particular group of people or the whole of humanity. We fear differences and this keeps us divided, or we are conditioned to think we are better because we are male, or because we are white, or British, or a human being, or whatever. All these divisions obviously exist; there is nothing wrong with things being different. The problems arise when we start making distinctions and divisions that separate us from others and that then become walls. We need boundaries, it is most important, but they should be the boundaries we choose rather than those imposed upon us – purposely or not – through individual or cultural or any other kind of conditioning. Positive boundaries, like skin, for example, are semi-permeable membranes, holding us in place but not acting as barriers to our free expression and interchange with the world, inside to outside or vice versa. Negative boundaries are walls that stop the free flow of information, experience or expression.

> *If schizophrenia is the disease of the human condition then polyphrenia, the orchestration and integration of our many selves, may be the health.*

> JEAN HOUSTON

We all play many parts in our lives. You might be a 'student' as you read this, then later become a 'daughter' while visiting your parents, then later still the 'avid partygoer' when you visit a friend's house. You might play the part of an 'angry old woman' when the right buttons are pushed, then a moment later be the 'cushion that everyone sits on'. Our personality is rather like an orchestra, and all these different parts of roles we play are like the players in that orchestra. As we become more able to define our lives, and control our processes in a positive inclusive way, we become like the conductor, allowing each individual member to play a part, and working towards orchestrating the personality into a harmonious whole. As the conductor we will also contact the composer who will supply us with information about how to play the musical composition of life and also, perhaps, information about each individual player's part in the whole.

Each of these parts of your personality – sometimes called 'subpersonalities' – knows what it wants and is determined to get it. They really care about themselves. This is okay, except that different parts can be in conflict. For example, part of you might want to eat a sticky cake, another part might want you to diet. To harmonise these different wants, it is necessary to get behind them to the deeper level of 'needs'. Needs are more inclusive than wants; 'I want you to kiss me right now' and 'I want to respect your own choice' might be conflicting wants. If I can tune into the underlying need – perhaps 'needing more affection in life generally' – then I can find ways to fulfil this need without coming into conflict.

One good way of achieving this shift from 'wanting' to 'needing' is through simply looking at what is happening and accepting it. You may come to accept that if you cannot get away from it you might as well include it. You need to get to know all your subpersonalities, build a relationship with them, love them in spite of their faults, give them space to grow. If you first recognise, then accept them, the required transformation will happen in its own way.

Roberto Assagioli, the founder of psychosynthesis, suggested naming each of our subpersonalities with humour, both as a way of connecting to their energies but also to maintain a healthy detachment and 'lightness' in this work. So, for example, a rather crazy emotional part of your personality could be called 'Larry Lupin'; a bossy part 'Mr Knowitall' and so on.

Wants are harsh and demanding, needs are more flexible. Wants are a behaviour pattern the subpersonality has learnt; needs are closer to the essence or quality, the core of the subpersonality. By moving towards needs you get to the quality, which is always inherently positive and trying to manifest. In the next exercise you will meet a subpersonality who will take you into a garden of roses. Enjoy the experience of this, and see how subpersonalities are not always in conflict, either with each other or with you.

Relax and centre.

Take a few deep breaths. Imagine you are in a meadow, and spend some time tuning into being there. What is the sky like? Is it a sunny day? How do you feel? What can you hear – birdsong perhaps? Smell? See? Really be in your meadow, as if it really exists.

In one direction you can see a small house or cottage. Walk that way, feeling your feet on the ground, and remembering to pay attention to being there. As you reach the house, you realise it is the home of some of your subpersonalities. You wonder who will live there, and how they will greet you. As you approach the door be aware of your excitement and anticipation.

You tap and the door is opened. Greet the person there, and pay attention to what he or she looks like. Is it a man or a woman or a child? Old or young? Fill in as much detail on this figure as you can. Then exchange some words, asking the figure its name if you like. Find out something about this person.

The subpersonality then asks you into the garden. It is a beautiful rose garden. Pay attention to the roses, their colours, scents, and overall beauty. Allow yourself to be infused with their quality. Walk with the subpersonality into the depths of the garden, then find one particular rose to which you are attracted.

Both you and the subpersonality look at this rose, brightly lit by a ray of sunshine. Feel the energy of the rose, its beauty and warmth, transform your feelings and thoughts. Really be whole, feeling good to be there at this time.

Then turn to the subpersonality and see how it has changed. Again engage him or her in dialogue and ask how he or she feels, what transformations, if any, may have taken place. Ask particularly about what the subpersonality needs.

Finally thank the subpersonality for taking you to the garden, say goodbye for now, and bring your consciousness back to your room. Write about the experience, and the needs of the subpersonality. In what way(s) can you express and fulfil this need, or at least some aspects of it in your daily life?

The Archetypal Energies

The four major archetypes that manifest through subpersonalities are Love, Will, Change and Maintenance. These archetypal energies create the pattern of existence as shown in Figure 4.

Love and Will are the two primary energies in conflict in a personality. They need to be unified. Each subpersonality plays out one of these archetypes – is it content with simply being, does it want to be loved, or does it want to do, to act, perhaps to control? When does it feel sad or hurt? Where does anger come from – your connection to love or your connection to will? It is important to find out the answers to these questions, but this is done most effectively through the overall process of your work rather than

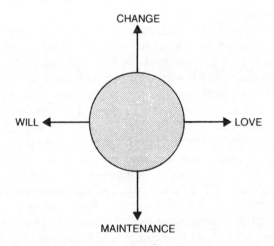

Figure 4: The Four Directions of Growth

through trying to mentally calculate answers. You have to watch particularly for 'complex layering' of these patterns. A certain part of you may feel angry, so you may think it a distortion of will energy, then you find it is really sad underneath and your orientation changes. Then perhaps underneath that it is angry again!

You can move a Love-orientated subpersonality toward unity by including it, listening to its needs, taking care of it.

A Will-orientated subpersonality is moved towards unity by expressing its needs, directing it clearly, letting it out from its restrictions in a harmonious way.

Of course, these parts have various ways of expressing their 'existential belief' and often this is very clear once they are encouraged to express their position. For example, a subpersonality might say: 'I won't be loved if I own my own power'; or 'I want to be perfect so everyone will love me'. Where do these subpersonalities fit into the dynamic of love and will?

Mal discovered a basic emotion-thinking conflict in her personality. An emotional subpersonality was always jealous, possessive and angry at the times her husband spent away from home with the group he played in. A mental part of her personality thought this was 'bad' and restrictive, and that she should not be so controlling. It wanted to eliminate the emotional part.

Dialoguing with the emotional part, Mal discovered it wanted attention. It also said it was too strong to 'be got rid of'. As she allowed this part to express itself, and to be nourished simply through being noticed, a transformation happened. A little bird popped into Mal's consciousness and, without words, it said to her it needed grounding, that she needed to love herself more, and to make more space for her own creative expression, not just her husband's. The little bird was expressing the real needs behind the possessive and jealous emotions Mal had originally been expressing. She took this little bird to her meadow, where it was very sunny. They went together to a mountain pool, and going into the water let the water and the sunshine caress them, opening and cleansing every pore of Mal's body. Afterwards she said it felt like 'loving myself completely for a moment'. It was the first time she had ever experienced this so fully. She looked really serene. The mental part now said it could accept the emotional part, and would try to help it develop.

It is wonderful how wise our inner processes can be once given the space to expand and integrate. Often we can see the unfoldment of Will energies through more mentally connected parts of our personality, and of the Love archetype through more emotional parts of ourselves. While this is generally true, however, it is not always the case: the Will can manifest through emotions and Love through the mind. Indeed, in some esoteric systems much is made of this 'crossing of the energies', whereby it is said a new, clearer understanding of the relationship between Love and Will can emerge and manifest.

The other two major archetypes, Change and Maintenance, create subpersonality types that either want everything (that affects them) to change, or everything to stay the same. These archetypes dynamically interact with the Love and Will archetypes. So, for example, you might have a Love-type subpersonality that wants change: 'everything would be better if only you would love me' or, on the other hand, one that does not want change, for instance: 'I couldn't live without you'. The interplay between the four archetypes of Love, Will, Change and Maintenance creates the arena in which we play out our relationship to the unfolding soul. The 'secret' is to co-operate with the process as much as possible – to choose or allow change when that is most appropriate, and to choose or allow stability when that is the wiser course. Both your ability to go with this process, and your resistances to the flow, are the source of the material you have to work with for the fullest manifestation of soul. You have to learn to trust in both things that change and in things that stay the same, and at the same time not be attached to either.

We can classify subpersonalities into three basic types or groups:

1. Those that are part of our core personality; parts we happily include as part of us, included in our sense of who we really are. Some of these are integrated, some co-operate with the process. They form the basis of the ego.

2. Suppressed subpersonalities; we know they are there but we do not accept them (for example, sexual drives, or self-assertion, which may become distorted then into an aggressive subpersonality). They are threatening to our sense of who we are, so not owned as part of who we are. They also include social conditioning, for instance, the 'topdog' who is always telling us what to do or not do. These subpersonalities are often projected on to other people.

3. Repressed subpersonalities; they are deep in the unconscious, primitive parts which are trapped and totally not accepted. They constitute what is sometimes called 'the shadow'.

Our aim is to expand our consciousness to include all three types. We can only transform subpersonalities when we connect with and fulfil their basic needs. Until then we remain fragmented, and this leads to the formation of defensive character styles. There are two simple categories of defence which can be found in either the suppressed or repressed subpersonality types mentioned above. Using Assagioli's advice, we can name them with 'loving humour':

'Vacant Vince'; he is split off, as if in trance, and is 'not at home'. Cut off from any true, direct experience, if he does express himself it is often through pleading for his wants in a very unbalanced way.

'Gimme Jimmy'; he finds his identity through others, always wants more, never has enough. He only knows where he stands when in relation to someone (or something) else; otherwise he feels lost, and will generally do anything in his power to avoid such a feeling.

The following examples are useful as suggestive descriptions of these types.

Sam had a subpersonality whom he described as 'a little boy called Sammy, he's an only child, a lonely child. If I become the centre of attention I become Sammy, it's a defence, 'cos as a little boy I can be silly and its okay. I'm not threatened then'. Sam needed to move to the qualities at the 'heart' of Sammy which he found to be honesty and openness. He was then able to disidentify from this part when he needed, and reidentify when he needed to do that too. He had the subpersonality rather than it having him.

Tom had a subpersonality he called 'Mrs Moanstone' who he described as 'a crabby, hypochondriac old woman'. In a guided visualisation she said to Tom: 'I need to be accepted for what I am. I need to be cared about. I have a man in my heart'. Tom walked her in the rose garden (see earlier exercise) and said he wished he knew the names of all the flowers that grow there. She responded in her usual crabby way: 'Don't worry about that, just enjoy them for what they are'. He saw for the first time some truth behind her crabbiness and tried to embrace her. She fought him off in a crabby but also loving sort of way! An introjection of his grandmother, he realised her quality as truth. When this happened her image transformed, became less wrinkled, and he saw her eyes for the first time – very clear and radiating truth. His physical body involuntarily shook at this moment, it was such a real communication, eye to eye with the loving truth-filled eyes of the woman he now renamed as 'Mrs Telltrue'.

Starhawk has said: 'community is the ultimate healer'. This is true on the inside as much as on the outside. Our inner community, our 'orchestra', as it grows and harmonises, becomes the ultimate healer of our divisions and fragmentation. The following exercise can help you see through some of your fragmentation and connect with layers of identification within your personality.

Relax and centre.

Sit comfortably and imagine you are an onion (yes, really!). What is your outer layer, your outer 'skin' like? Spend some time considering this.

Then imagine this outer skin is peeled off. What is your next layer like?

Continue peeling off more layers of your onion, looking at each in turn, until you reach the very core. What is this like?

Andrew did this exercise and found six layers in his 'onion'. The first, outer skin, he described as 'fat and stupid'. Next was a layer he said was filled with experiences, and felt like 'a concentration camp'. Behind this was a little boy, a 'soldier and a scholar'. Next inside he found a layer that was 'a little baby that was somehow a foetus and an old man in one'. The next layer he experienced as like 'being afloat in outer space', and then the innermost layer he could access was a rolling black cloud. Andrew said there were more layers beneath this but for now he could not reach them.

There is no 'right' level to reach, nothing wrong with finding you can go no deeper towards your core. What is important is to honour your own processes and, as your layers are peeled back, to recognise and own what you find underneath. That way you are co-operating with the process of your personal evolution.

· 6 ·

CHOOSING TO BE HERE
Exploring Perception

The world is as it looks and yet it isn't. It's not as solid and real as our perception has led us to believe, but it isn't a mirage either . . . something out there is affecting our senses.

CARLOS CASTANEDA

What we imagine is there is what we are seeing only after we have filtered it through the walls we have built around our perceptions. This is true for all the senses, not just seeing. It is also true of feelings, and even our thoughts. We are constantly choosing to only sense some things, and to filter out other things. Just now I heard a blackbird start singing outside; for a moment all I could hear was the bird song. All other sounds went into a vacuum, as it were. Then a car passed the front of the house and the spell was broken. Remember a time when something like this happened to you recently.

After we have chosen what we sense, we then pass it through the filters that have been imprinted, or conditioned into us. These filters are effective for all perceptions, including feelings. They are created when we are told things as children, such as 'be a good girl and help mummy with the washing'. Equated: being a good girl, doing the washing.

'I've told you before, you can't do that'. And each time it is repeated it is believed that much more, until we take it as our own idea. We believe we cannot do it, even when it is something we really could do, if we just believed that instead. We are really a mess of badly interpreted messages filtered through an out-of-date filter that only picks up a small percentage of what it is able to pick up when working efficiently!

This sounds awful, but we can easily start to deal with this, and improve the situation. This chapter is about exploring perception, and is chiefly composed of little exercises and suggestions that can aid you to do just that. Awareness is fun – it is, after all, what separates the 'living' from the 'dead'! So enjoy this chapter and let yourself have fun while exploring the exercises. It is undoubtedly true that something which excites and interests you has more effect than something which you find boring or uninteresting.

We can start with an exercise that helps you tune into your awareness in a very simple but effective way.

Relax and centre.

Using the words: 'Now I am aware . . .' to start each time, voice out loud whatever you are aware of and watch how your awareness is constantly changing.

For example: now I am aware of my fingers on the keyboard . . . now I am aware of three little dots . . . now I am aware of feeling warm and bright . . . now I am aware of the sunshine . . . now I am aware of my lips being dry . . . now I am aware of . . .

Try this 'awareness continuum' for several minutes. Persist for a little while after you feel like stopping – sometimes the most interesting connections are made when you 'push' yourself a little.

Now do it again for a few minutes more, this time noticing what stops your awareness. Are there moments when nothing seems to come? Do you feel it is all pointless, or does it make you feel a little embarrassed to do it out loud?

Now do it once more, this time paying attention to how your awareness changes from inside to outside awareness, and vice versa.

This awareness continuum is composed of our intuitions, thoughts, feelings, emotions, sensations, imaginings – all the parts of our total being.

We can also project our awareness into other things. When Jo realised this for the first time she was sitting in her favourite armchair in front of a gas fire. She tried it out: 'I am a gas fire. I convert one form of energy into another. When I am turned on I please and warm people. When I am turned off I am forgotten. I am a transmitter of energy and my whole existence depends upon being in receipt of the energy I convert. One day I will no longer perform my function and I shall be redundant scrap; but the energy I transmit will still exist'.

Now you try it out. Choose some inanimate object in your room and project your awareness into it. Do not think about it, judge or censor what you say, just allow yourself to speak as if you were that object.

It is possible to become totally absorbed in otherness. Pat projected herself into another country! 'I am an American city. Watch out! I am full of life, teeming, sharp and slick. The night is my time, I throb and sparkle. My allies slide through me. I am concrete ground. My heart is black. Rush, fight, survive . . . alive!'

It is also possible to project yourself into parts of your body, which is very useful for healing. You can also project yourself into parts of your personality, which is what you were doing in the last chapter when dealing with subpersonalities.

The next exercise brings a sense of being 'new born' in that you can start connecting with the freshness and 'newness' of any situation you are in without becoming identified or attached to what is happening.

Relax and centre.

With your eyes closed, be as relaxed and empty of thoughts, feelings and sensations as possible.

When you feel ready, open your eyes and see the world before you, wherever you are, as a completely new place.

Everything and everyone you see is not named. You have no mental, emotional or physical constructs with which to identify your environment. You are not attached to anything.

Imagine yourself as a new-born being.

Now go back into your inner space, still self-identified, and make a clear decision that when you open your eyes again, you will see everything and everyone else as equally reborn. Everything has its old familiar name, but is different, new, seen in a new light because of your choice for it to be so.

Open your eyes.

There is a 'wall of nightmares' which exists in the 'space' or 'zone' or even 'world' between your initial perception and what response there is inside you to that perception. It is possible to explore this 'nightmare' without becoming so attached that you slip into it and become trapped by fear. The next exercise achieves just this.

Relax and centre.

Look around you, choose anything in your room, and say 'I see . . .' whatever it is. Still looking at it, say 'I imagine . . .' and let yourself make whatever connection comes to that object. Then say 'I feel . . .' and see what your inner feeling is at this moment.

Repeat this procedure a few times with different objects, each time saying 'I see', 'I imagine', 'I feel'.

It is quite interesting doing this with another person, looking at one another and alternating turns of using the three statements. Or try it subvocally when in the company of other people and notice the differences between what you see, what you imagine as a result of that seeing, and what you are feeling inside.

Three components of this exercise clearly differentiate between the reality of perception (what you see), the reality of your actual response (what you feel) and what comes between, what you imagine – the 'nightmare'. Of course, it is not always negative or intrusive, it can be a nice dream rather than a nightmare, but it still separates you from direct perception of your world. And it becomes a definite nightmare when it includes insertions between perception and reality that cause you to see things only through the filter of this particular wall. This wall is composed of many things, but primary amongst its bricks are: explaining, imagining, interpreting, guessing, thinking, comparing, planning, remembering the past, and anticipating the future.

Relax and centre.

Watch your breath without changing the rhythm, just let it go in and out, out and in in a flowing cycle. Then let thoughts and images emerge in your consciousness. Do not try to stop them, let them emerge and appear to you. Let them do what they want, to change, merge, give you messages, whatever. Just do not get attached. Remain as an observer of these images and thoughts. See them come, and see them go.

After several minutes start paying attention to the spaces between these images and thoughts. They may only be very tiny spaces but they will exist, and you will see them if you look for them. Then realise that the images and thoughts that usually seem to be continuously there are not continuous; they come and go. Your inner dialogue and your inner screen can both be turned off. You pay attention and choose the spaces between.

The spaces between thoughts are just as real as the thoughts. You are still there, experiencing. You can choose this silence as readily as you can choose the noise of thoughts. One is not better than the other, as such, but both have value and you usually pay little or no attention in life to inner silence. Now, give the silence a voice – what does it say to you? The voice of silence is sometimes esoterically called 'the voice of the swan'.

The 'sound of silence' can be difficult to hear, but so can the 'sound of sounds' which is surrounding you at all times. Yet it is possible to 'just listen' without doing anything with what you hear.

Relax and centre.

With eyes closed, listen to the sounds around you. Watch how you categorise and name these sounds: it is a car, a bird, etc.

Now listen to the sounds and try not to name or categorise them, just listen to them for what they are. Imagine the sounds as expressions of pure energy you are receiving and are able to hear in its pure form. You do not need to interpret or anything. Just listen in . . .

Notice how the sounds come to you, notice how they enter you. Is it always through the ears? Do some sounds seemingly pass you by, while others really grab your attention? Pay attention to the wall of sounds around you.

Let this experience really take you over, become one with the sounds around you.

The more effectively you do this, the more you can really let yourself be, and the more you let yourself be, the more you are able to do what you want.

Remember something from your past that feels good, has positive and pleasant associations. Take some time really recalling this time in detail. Play the part of an interested and involved observer, but do not get carried away by the pleasure.

Now remember something from the past that is unpleasant. Again take some time recalling this incident in detail, playing the part of an interested and involved observer without getting caught up in the painful or unpleasant memories.

How is awareness of the two different?

Often we find that, after something unpleasant, there are blocks, holes or 'interruptions' in the flow of awareness, which keep the memories at a distance. Mike's father and mother had a row and the father was leaving the house in a very angry mood. Mike's mother asked him to stop his father leaving. 'If you want him to stay,' she said, 'you'd better stop him.' Mike actually did this, and his father did stay, but whatever had happened at that time, it created a moment in Mike's past that he could not face. He was trapped by this structure, by this 'hole in his memory' until he remembered it and restructured it through visualisation.

Focus now on a moment of awareness just before the painful or negative memory. Using your imagination to its fullest, allow yourself to connect with this, then simply change the perception. Let it emerge as you would have chosen it.

For example, when Mike restructured the incident above, he imagined his grandfather came and sorted his mother and father out. The fact that his grandfather was actually dead at that time was not relevant, and no way reduced the efficacy of his intervention!

Fritz Perls said: 'Anxiety is the tension between the now and the later. The gap is a void that usually is filled with planning, predictions, expectations. . . habitual repetitions'. The Gestalt teacher Judith Brown tells the story of a young man who once saw a beautiful woman ride past on a horse and became obsessed with her. He wanted to make love to her so much he could not stop thinking about her all day long. For days he waited at the same time on the same road and watched her ride by. Yet he was too shy and nervous to say anything to her.

Then he devised a plan: 'I'll follow her back to the stables, then when she has left, I'll sneak in and paint a blue circle on the backside of her horse. Then tomorrow when she rides past, I'll have something to say to her. I'll shout. "There's a blue circle on the back of your horse, miss" and offer to clean it off for her. And she'll be grateful, and we'll talk, and she'll get off her horse, and we'll talk some more, then she'll smile at me and I'll ask her out. Then that night, we'll go out and at the end of the evening we'll have a passionate kiss. Then the next day we'll . . .' and so his fantasising continued until he got to a week later and they eventually make love.

So he did what he had fantasised, followed her and painted the circle on her horse. The next day as she rode past, he shouted to her, 'Excuse me, there's a blue circle on the back of your horse'.

'I know,' she responded, jumping down off her horse. 'Let's fuck!'

Trust in your own perceptions. A Sufi initiate taught himself to walk on water by chanting the word 'zumzah'. He walked on the river outside his house every day on his way to a friend's house. One day a famous Sufi master was passing, saw him on the water, heard his chanting and shouted: 'Hey, Brother Sufi, you are saying it wrong. It is not "zumzah", it should be "zahzum"'.

'Thank you,' replied the initiate, changing his chant to 'zahzum'. At which point he immediately sank!

Sometimes we can alter perceptions through mirroring what we perceive. Andy was excusing some behaviour of his, and looked like he was not really present. His hands were all over the place, and his chest was sunken. I mirrored him and he said it made him feel embarrassed, like a game was being played with him. I persisted. His voice became a little squeaky sound. I asked him to exaggerate it, then to move his body with each squeak. As he did so his head moved back each time, while his hips and upper legs thrust outwards. The more he did it, the more energy was raised, and the more he was patently enjoying it, although he said it made him feel 'naughty'. I encouraged him to persist, and to exaggerate it more. As he did so, his body moved faster and more involuntarily, until he let out an ear-piercing scream. And he laughed and laughed, in a deeper, more full way than ever before.

Try mirroring some little children, and watch their reaction. It is great fun!

Lucid Dreaming

Not all our awareness takes place when we are awake, for we can also be aware in dreams. The greatest awareness at this time comes when we are fortunate enough to have a lucid dream. Lucid dreaming is different from ordinary dreaming in that, in the former, you can make deliberate acts. It is as if you become conscious within a dream that you are dreaming, but rather than awakening, you find you can choose to remain in the dream and affect its course. There are many methods for lucid dreaming. Perhaps the simplest is to tell yourself, as you drop off to sleep, that you are a lucid dreamer! Such an affirmation is implanted in your unconscious and helps create the conditions in which lucid dreaming can happen. You cannot expect it to happen every time, however, and you may need to repeat the formula continuously for many weeks or months before success is achieved.

Another technique is to watch for the beginning of images that tell you a dream is commencing; then, with clear awareness and determination, choose to look at your hands. This may sound very difficult and it certainly is not easy, but if you persist it does work. You can practise this technique and the practice in itself helps set up the conditions for it to happen during dreaming. You practise through allowing yourself to daydream, then remembering to hold your hands before you and looking at them. Then shift your gaze from the hands to whatever objects are in your dream and fix your gaze on them instead. Alternating between focusing on your hands and the images before you, continue this until you sense the dream is ready to move on, then consciously choose the next unfoldment of the action. When you sense yourself becoming unconscious, simply hold your arms out and look at your hands once more.

Even if lucidity does not come, however, it is always useful to watch dreams, looking particularly for patterns in the events of dreams that help us understand our relationship to our unconscious. Watching – and recording – our dreams also increases perception. When we realise that we spend a third of our life in sleep, it becomes almost second nature to accept that the events we remember from 'dreamtime' are worthy of our attention. Dreams are direct messages from your unconscious. They are your nightly 'astral trips', so take the time and space to enjoy them, to use them, not to interpret them in some dry psychological way, or in some 'mystical' way, but just to live with them and deal with them as events in your whole life that are just as real as the events in your 'waking' life.

Relax and centre.

Imagine you are driving a car down a long, straight road. You start thinking about what happened last night. Think now about what really did occur in your life last night. Remember the events in detail, and allow any feelings that are there to emerge freely.

Now think of somewhere you could be going on your car journey. Perhaps you are on your way to visit a friend you have not seen for some time. Think what you might say to him or her. Imagine the warm, friendly reception you will receive when you arrive. Think of the food you might be offered, and so on. Give your imagination free rein and go into the fantasy you create.

Now recall the road you are travelling down. Who was driving while you were away?

Anything you do or say either takes you towards or away from the fulfilment of your goals. You choose what you create in your world. How you feel is not a result of what is happening but is the result of your interpretation of what is happening. A film director could produce many different films from the same situation; someone falling off a ladder, for example, may be funny or sad. You have a similar power over your world. If you really believe you cannot fail in anything you do, how can you fail?

Relax and centre.

Remember something from your past about which you were strongly motivated and which you successfully achieved. It does not have to be any big thing, just something, however small, which you achieved with complete success.

Remember the associated events with as much clarity as possible – really see the images, hear and feel what happened to the fullest possible degree.

Now think of something you want to be strongly motivated to do in your life. Again see it, hear it and feel it as vividly as possible.

Now transfer the qualities of the first incident from the past to this new wished-for happening. See the future event with the same light, with the same brightness and quality that is associated with your past success.

Realise you have the power to make it happen.

After so many exercises which have been exploring perception in action, we will finish this chapter with a silent meditation. Whatever you experience, it is always 'you' at the centre of the experience. You are the perceiver and, at your core, you are filled with an endless source of energy that is both dynamic and exciting, yet at the same time sublimely silent.

Relax and centre.

Pay attention to the rhythmic flow of your breathing without trying to change it or force it in any way. Just let yourself freely and easily breathe for a while.

Say to yourself: 'My body is at peace'. Be aware of any sensations in your body but do not try to suppress them in any way.

Next affirm silently to yourself: 'My emotions and feelings are at peace'. Do not suppress any emotions that arise, simply be aware of them and let them pass.

Then silently affirm: 'My thoughts are at peace'. Notice whatever thoughts arise but do not become attached to them.

Visualise yourself as perfectly silent. Be at peace in a perfectly silent, peaceful world.

Silently affirm: 'I have sensations, emotions, feelings, thoughts, but I, as an individual soul, am eternally at peace and at one with the universal rhythm'.

Realise the truth of this statement.

Sometimes my experience of the world tells me it is all a
    muddy, unclear and distorted reflection,
But then when I am still inside, the waters clear and I see
    that outside me is inside me and inside me is outside me,
For then I let things come, let things be, let things go.

If sometimes you can see me just simply being me,
And sometimes I can see you just simply being you,
Then we have scraped off a little of the silver
    on the mirror between us:
Perhaps one day it will all be gone
    and through the clear glass
We will see us just simply being us.

These words are a ripple in the water,
So watch with me as the water settles again,
And know the silence that is more than silence, for it is joy.

WILL PARFITT (May, 1979)

· 7 ·

CHANGING YOUR WORLD
Exploring Imagination

> *We sin against the imagination whenever we ask an image for its meaning, requiring that images be translated into concepts.*
>
> JAMES HILLMAN

Symbols are the language of the unconscious. They are the 'life' of myths, dreams, images and everything that is 'created in' or 'received into' your imagination. Through symbols everything is imagined. We create our experience through symbols, making it what we want it to be. But to be able to undertake such transformations of our experience, we need to be able to contact our unconscious, the 'home', as it were, of symbols. Paradoxically, to do this we use symbols!

One way of gaining access to the unconscious is through the symbols and imagery in stories, tales and myths, particularly those that can touch the deeper levels within us. This is the art of story-telling, to reach into the depths of the listener and place symbols there that affect thoughts, feelings and even sensations.

A little bird was captured by a hunter. The bird told the hunter that he would swap three pieces of invaluable advice in return for being set free. After much deliberation, the hunter agreed to this proposal.

The first piece of advice from the bird was to not hold onto things, to let things come and let things go. The hunter thought this was good advice and let the bird out of his hand.

The second piece of advice was to trust in what you directly sense and experience. The hunter thought this was good advice and let the bird fly to a nearby tree.

As soon as this happened, the little bird flew off, laughing wildly. The man shouted to the bird, asking him what was so funny, to which the bird responded: 'if only you had known I had within me the largest most precious jewel in the world you would never have let me go.' And he laughed all the more.

This made the hunter very angry and he shouted to the bird, screaming for him to come back. The bird ignored this. 'Well at least keep your bargain,' the man said, 'and give me the last piece of advice'.

'Why should I do that for you, foolish man,' replied the bird, 'when you didn't pay attention to my first two pieces of advice. You are not letting things come and go, look at the way you are getting all worked up trying to get me back. And you didn't trust your senses otherwise you would realise a little bird like me couldn't possibly have the largest most precious jewel in the world inside my tiny body!' The bird laughed, and turned to fly off. 'Look,' he said, 'as you didn't act upon my first two pieces of advice, I'm not going to waste a third piece of precious wisdom on you'. And with that he flew away.

The bird did give the man a third piece of advice, the best of all, namely that good advice is pointless unless you act upon it. It seems doubtful that the man heeded this any more than he took notice of the first two pieces of advice.

Tales offer a symbolic connection to the unconscious. They can connect us to our feelings and to the processes in our unconscious. These feelings and processes can then be transformed through the reification of the characters, objects, ideas, or whatever that they represent. They allow us to understand our inner wisdom in a stimulating way, stimulating the imagination and offering new possibilities. Tales help our understanding to increase in a dynamic way, giving us messages we need to be able to function effectively in life. They can help underdeveloped parts of ourselves come out and gain independence. Tales are reassuring, partly through allowing us to regress and tread again old paths to ensure our continuity, and through giving reassurance about the transitions we go through, for example, from the safe family environment to the outer, 'dangerous world' situation. Tales not only offer a symbolic connection, they can also transform our relationship with the unconscious.

Imagery

In this book there are lots of exercises that use guided imagery. There are many ways to use imagery, mainly for exploring the unconscious. Imagery can act as a laboratory of life so to speak, somewhere to try things out in a symbolic way. For instance, things that frighten us can be accessed and worked on before the actual situation (for example, an interview) happens. This can include fantasies as well as real fears.

Through images, it is also possible to contact archetypal symbols, and manifest them in the everyday world. For example, contacting joy and manifesting it could be nothing but positive in its effect on the planet. Symbols can help us discover our power, including new and different ways to interact with the world and to use our will, to be able to choose what we want to choose, and say no to that which we reject. Discrimination is a positive quality which comes through true owning of power.

So how do you use imagery for these effects? You can start, for example, with a given image, like the meadow or the mountain found in some of the exercises in this book. Or you could have an unfolding daydream based on a particular suggestion like the 'onion peelings exercise' in Chapter 5. You could imagine looking into a crystal ball.

Imagery can also be completely unstructured, just letting it unfold, to see what happens. Tom imagined he was in a cave, and waited to see what would happen. To his surprise, a vulva-shaped hole opened in one wall of the cave, and he could see a woodland scene outside. Climbing through the hole, Tom found himself in a sunlit glade near a little brook that seemed to bubble up from a spring. Having explored the area, he decided to follow the brook and see what happened. He had many adventures along the way as the brook became a stream which became a small river, then a larger and larger river until it reached the sea. At the sea he swam out, became totally immersed in the water, let himself surrender to the sensation, and, becoming a piece of driftwood, he was washed up on a sandy beach. He believed he was dead. Then a beautiful young goddess with the sun in her eyes arrived and breathed new life into him. He revived, feeling strong and newly born. He remembered his journey from the dark cave and felt so grateful for the experience he sang praises to his inner, 'higher' Self.

We might think Tom's experience was something to do with life and death, or with the actual birth experience perhaps. However we interpret it – correctly or incorrectly – there is no doubt it was a powerful experience which had a very transforming effect on his life. Yet what was it, but imagination?

Whatever kind of imagery you are using, you are building a bridge from the conscious to the unconscious, you are changing the wall between those two states into what you choose it to be, with the bricks or blocks ordered as you want to put them, rather than in an order imposed upon you through design, accident, or through blind conditioning.

It is important to connect images and symbols with your body, and conversely to use your body as a source of symbols and images. How is your body right now? You can use it as a starting place, watch for images that emerge and use them creatively. Or you can breathe into your body to release any negative, embedded images that create the 'armouring' that you might find in the muscles and tissues that make you up.

Relax and centre.

Imagine you are a house. See yourself as a house. What kind of house are you – a cottage, a terraced house, a grand mansion or what? Take some time to imagine what sort of house you are in as much detail as possible.

Picture this house in front of you and imagine you enter through the front door. This is no problem, for it is your house. You can explore the rest of the house some other time, but for now we will visit the basement or cellar.

Find the way down to the basement, and consider what it is like. Go into as much detail as you can, from assessing the condition of the foundations, the walls of the basement, the damp level, what junk might be stored there, and so on. Assess whatever comes up so you get a good, clear picture of the full state of your basement. Really be as honest as if you were a surveyor checking the house for possible purchase.

Now recall it is your house and you can choose to do with it whatever you like. Change the basement in any way that seems suitable to you. Perhaps you need to reinforce the walls, or dry it out, or paint it, or throw away junk – take some time to make your basement into the sort of basement you would most like to have.

The power of your imagination will even allow you to add or remove rooms, completely change the shape or style of the basement, make of it what you will.

Free Drawing

'Free drawing' allows you the chance to be expressive without worrying about what you are going to express. To do the following exercise in free drawing, take a large piece of paper and a pencil or pen with which you like to write.

Relax and centre.

Sit in front of the paper, and start drawing. Do not think about it consciously, just let the images and pictures unfold, so that what you draw comes straight from you without judgements or ideas imposed upon it. Let your hands do whatever they choose to do.

Try doing some drawing with the hand you do not usually use. Allow your expression free rein.

When you have finished, look over your drawing and see what you can find in it. Are there symbols? Do parts of it look like something – faces, animals, clouds, whatever? Look at the textures, lines, shapes, forms, colours, anything that catches your eye. You can fill in bits on the drawing at this stage, to make the things you see in it become more real. A cleverly placed eye can make a face really come alive.

Such drawing helps to mobilise your energy, breaks down old, unnecessary control, and is a means of expressing yourself. Free drawing can also be a dis-identifying experience if you really let yourself go with the pen. If it has not worked well this time, practise it more, perhaps with longer or deeper meditation before starting.

We dealt in the last chapter with lucid dreaming. Here we are more concerned with the symbolic content of dreams, which can be worked on in various ways. For example:

- Gestalt dialoguing; try taking an item, a person or an inanimate object or anything, from your dream, and have a conversation with this item, let it speak and give you information of use to you.

- Consciously continuing with the contents; if a dream feels incomplete in any way, allow yourself to imagine what happens next, let the 'story' of the dream unfold until it comes to a positive, life-enhancing conclusion.

- Drawing, or painting images from dreams; this can be most useful, and give you real insights into the meaning of your dreams without imposing false or dubious 'intellectual interpretations' on the content. Free drawing after holding a powerful image from a dream can be most interesting.

- Recognising recurring themes in dreams, whether whole scenes or just little items of content, can be useful in helping you see things that you are attached to or which you need to work on in some way.

The Essence of Symbols

It is a real joy to mould the content of your unconscious, to control it in a positive way, rather than letting it control you. This is true 'psychological craftsmanship.'

Relax and centre.

Let a positive image emerge from your unconscious, see it, hear it, feel it, then let it grow bigger and bigger, let it overwhelm you and feel its positive energy.
Then let a negative image emerge from your unconscious, see it, hear it, feel it, then let it grow smaller and smaller until it disappears, burnt up in an imaginary sun.

These images, positive or negative, are always emerging. You can react to them or you can act upon them, you can have them or let them have you. If you have them then you can do what you want with them – feeding on the positive ones, making them bigger and stronger, dispersing the negative ones, not letting them take you over.

There are five basic ways to get deeper into the essence of a symbol:

1.   Objective consideration of its form, what it shows you on its surface. To do this you simply use your senses – without interpreting or judging the symbol in any way, simply look at it and see what understanding you can find in its basic form.

2.   Experiencing it emotionally, allowing the feelings it brings up full play in your conscious experience. This is using your feeling function to help you understand the symbol, again without judgement or interpretation. How does it make you feel? What value can you find in this symbol?

3.   Penetrating more deeply to its meaning, using your intellectual skills to discover what it teaches you. Using your thinking function, you can bring your knowledge into play and interpret the symbol as clearly as you are able.

4.   Grasping the abstract meaning of the symbol, letting its inner or deeper meaning come to you intuitively. Behind all the sensations, feelings and thoughts you may have about the symbol is its more abstract, 'bigger' meaning, an understanding that goes beyond your individual concepts about it. You cannot learn to be intuitive, you can only 'let it happen'.

5.   Identifying with the symbol, to discover its quality and purpose, to connect with its 'soul'. The form in which the symbol manifests may obscure its deepest meaning or it may not, but in either case, through identifying yourself with the symbol you can start to connect with its deepest essence. To do this effectively you have to be centred and relaxed, and not attached to any of the thoughts, feelings or even intuitions you may already have about it.

It is possible to change both the fantasy world and the reality of life on an individual and collective level. The symbols you have to work with need never be suggested from outside, as your unconscious will invariably send you the right messages. You can trust these messages from your inner world, and act upon them in a transformative way.

In a guided fantasy, Susie reached the top of a mountain and found a stone altar there. On top of the altar was a pool of water, and inside the pool was a little, jewelled box. Susie trusted the process, and decided to open the box. When she did so, she saw an emerald ring inside, and she understood she could wear the ring and it would protect her when she felt anger. Susie had had problems with expressing a lot of bottled-up anger, that tended to come out in inappropriate ways. After this experience, she discovered that by imagining herself wearing the ring, she could trust that it was okay to express her anger when it was appropriate, and not to do so when that was the case.

Realise how it is possible to shake off negative energies – for example, resentment at time spent doing something, or envy, or prejudice, or whatever. Maybe after a long day at the office, you could change clothes and in so doing shake off the unpleasant and put on the new, the fresh, the chosen items that bring you chosen happenings. It is always your choice. You might say clothes are actual things, not symbols, but the clothes you wear for any particular role you play have a symbolic function. If you remove your 'uniform' you remove the 'symbols' of your role. People have many different ways for changing their psychic connections, but, in whatever way we do it, there is a real need. We can find ways of succeeding that are not only harmless but even beneficial, both to ourselves and other people, particularly those with whom we are in close contact.

This has real political implications, for as the individual changes so there is change to the collective, and it is through such changes that we can begin the manifestation of a new, positive attitude and action in the world, rather than succumbing to the numbing reality that there are people out there who would control us and make of us less than we have the potential to be.

· 8 ·

MATTER AND MATRIX
Exploring the Body

Here in the body are the sacred rivers; here are the sun and moon, as well as the pilgrimage places. I have not encountered another temple as beautiful as my own body.

[ANCIENT TANTRIC TEXT]

In a previous chapter when you worked on changing your relationship to a particular discomfort in your body, you were entering the deepest recesses of your living temple, your body. You were delving into what, on one level, seems the most outward manifestation of your existence, and yet is, in another sense, the place of your most intimate, deepest secrets. For you inhabit your body and nowhere else. So long as you are alive on this planet it is true to say everything you experience is in your body.

Relax and centre.

Be aware of how much space you fill up with your body, right up to the very edge of your skin. Really feel yourself occupying your own physical space. Then tune inside to the space within, and imagine it as limitless.

John had the following experience the second time he did this exercise. 'I feel full up inside. . . something grips me, not bad, but I feel gripped, around my neck, an inside feeling pushing outwards, making it feel gripped. . . I want to be inside to be more outside. . . I feel I have to be outside. . . but I feel I have to go inside to get the strength to come outside, I need more nourishment from inside. . . something frightens me inside although I enjoy it once I'm there. . . I'm frightened, but I'm interested too, there's an enormous space and I'm looking round inside it, peering around looking for the something I'm frightened of, and when I look there really isn't anything to be frightened of, I'm fine, the space is fine. . . when I first close my eyes I get a feeling of fear then after a while it is okay – and this is true when I'm first outside too. I can easily become attached to either, now I'm inside I really don't want to come out, I have to really consciously choose to open my eyes'.

It is possible to see your body as a temple, then to explore the various parts of this temple. The following exercise assists you in doing just that.

Relax and centre.

Tune into various places in your body, your temple. Go first to your feet, and look at the relationship between your feet and the external world, your contact with matter.

Tune into your hands, again paying attention to the relationship between them and your world. Then travel to your belly and see what relationship you have there, then to your face, being aware of the many muscles that make up your face, and the shapes and patterns in your face.

Finally travel to your heart, the sacred centre of your temple, and tune in there. Feel the radiating light from your heart fill up your whole body, until you are glowing with its health-giving presence.

The following exercise, which is in two parts, is very powerful. Take your time and only go as far as you feel able. Do not push and the energy will flow of itself.

Relax and centre.

Look at yourself naked in a mirror, and have a dialogue with who you see. Share mutually and deeply with this other person as if he or she were your very closest, most intimate friend.

Then imagine the image in the mirror is your 'double', that part of you that lives in the subtler realms of existence. Let energy flow between you and your double, for you can heal each other by tuning in and letting energy flow freely between you.

Breathing

The main way we interact with our world is through breathing. If we do not do it, we stop, and if we continue not to do it, we die. Breathing is our primary interface with the outside. We take in air, and we breathe it back out, changed in the obvious ways regarding oxygen and carbon dioxide, but also in subtler ways. You can affect both what you take in and what you put out. For instance, you can choose to breathe deeply when you are at the ocean, or in a forest filled with clean, fresh air. You can affect how you breathe in or out, too. If you are in the presence of something you find unpleasant in some direct physical way, you can choose to breathe in and out very fast, short breaths, and this protects you on an energy level from being 'contaminated' by the unpleasantness.

How you affect what you put out when you exhale is more subtle and yet, in a way, even more powerful. You can use your imagination to put anything you like into your out-breath. Why not choose now to breathe out all your aches and pains, all that is 'out of sync' in your body?

Despite all this, we usually take our breathing for granted. It has been said if you breathe more slowly you will live longer; perhaps this is true, because animals like mice who breathe fast live much shorter lives than animals that breathe slowly, such as reptiles. But whether this is true or not, it is of utmost importance to breathe as fully and clearly as you can without forcing it at all. It is also of interest to investigate within yourself the space between breaths, that is, the space after you have breathed out fully and not yet started to breathe in, and vice versa. By focusing on these spaces, and using them as contact points with your unconscious, you can vitalise your whole physical world.

Many systems of yoga and meditation suggest ways of breathing that require you to breathe in particular patterns. You might be asked to breathe in for a count of 8, hold your breath for a count of 4, then breathe out for a count of 16, then hold on out for 8. This would be called a 8:4:16:8 cycle. Each particular cycle is said to bring a particular healing, or confer a particular power upon the practitioner. The experience of people who try this out is usually very positive, and so long as nothing is forced rarely, if ever, harmful.

What is perhaps of most importance is the consciousness such cyclical breathing brings to bear. When you breath more consciously you generally become more harmonious in your life and your body's energy strengthens. You can breathe into different parts of your body by putting a hand on the place where you wish to focus. Try breathing into your belly, then into your chest, then try to take your breath down to your lower belly, your genital area, then right up into your throat. By breathing to different places you can create different effects. Generally the best way to breathe is relaxedly but fully, filling the belly, then the chest, then just letting the tension this creates, the vacuum, push the air back out without any effort whatsoever. It is also advisable generally to breathe in through the nose.

The diaphragm is the only place in the body where we have direct access to our autonomic nervous system through the central nervous system. In other words, by controlling our breathing, and changing its patterns, we can directly affect our autonomic nervous system. Amongst other things, the autonomic nervous system is involved with functions in the thoracic vessels, the abdominal viscera, the pelvic organs and the glands. Heart rate is an example of a function directly controlled by this system. It is also involved in the functioning of your emotions. To be able to tune into this system is therefore of great use and benefit to the individual.

Never overdo breathing exercises, just go to your limits. You will find these limits will expand of their own accord without your having to push them. Most people never reach their limits, but are happy to remain in a state of poorly held breathing, not aware of the cycles and strength of breathing at all. Try breathing in positive energy, holding your breath and feel it filling your whole body. Then breathe out negative energy, until there is no breathe left within you, and experience that completeness before repeating the cycle. Do this smoothly, without jerking your breath or your body, and it will be very beneficial.

The following are ways of experiencing breathing in a new way, and putting more consciousness into the process. They can be used singly or in combination, and can easily be adapted for use by a couple. Remember, as with all breathing techniques, not to push beyond what you sense to be your limit, that in itself is enough to remove a brick from the wall of limitation.

1.   Watch for the space between breaths, both the space when breath is all out (at the end of your exhalation), and the space when breath is all in (at the end of your inhalation). Concentrate on those spaces and allow them to fill with a bright, white light.

2.   Centre on these spaces between breathing and, within them, find yourself.

3.   At any moment, stop and pay attention to either of the spaces. As you start to breathe again, feel re-born.

4.   Centre on those spaces between breathing and, within them, lose yourself.

5.   In the spaces between breaths, in that very space experience total unlimited energy.

The Dragon Power

Most traditions, east and west, tell of a special power within our bodies, called the dragon power, the snake, kundalini, shakti or shekhinah. It is a power closely linked to our sexual energy and is sometimes described as a snake coiled at the base of the spine that uncoils and stretches up through the body as the energy is activated. It is also described as a dragon power that resides at the base of the clitoris or penis, that similarly rises up through the body. It is considered dangerous to raise this power prematurely, but it is important that you start to build a relationship with it.

Relax and centre.

Tune into the base of your penis or clitoris, and imagine
there is a power there. Imagine an animal – whatever
animal comes to you, and see this animal as your helper.
Let it speak to you, or move, or show you in some way
something of its relationship to you at this moment. Really
get to know it and love it and cherish it. Then when it is
ready to rise, whatever the situation, it will do so naturally,
and you will be without fear.

When this energy is activated it brings an inner excitement,
a joyous thrilling sensation throughout the body, taking the
breath away. It can move mountains! It is sometimes referred
to in this way in the descriptions of very exciting sexual
encounters. This is a true mystical experience, of connectedness
with universal energy. It is not a substitute or 'dangerous short
cut' but an experience, available to every man and every woman,
that allows them to experience themselves as living centres of
energy, as 'stars' no less. By following their true course through
the heavens, stars are not bounded by walls and are free to
express themselves in their own, individual and unique way.

You can have this experience, but do not try to do anything
with it beyond letting it infuse you with its strength, and cleanse
you. It can really transform your life, but do not push it too hard,
it must come as it comes. You can truly connect to the mystical
love energy and fully understand why all the best mystics have
maintained that love is the central, overriding energy in the
universe.

*It is our birthright to walk through walls. The molecular
structure of our bodies is light. At this time we're vibrating
very very slowly.*

CHRIS GRISCOM

In a later chapter we will look into the faster vibrational states,
but for now realise the truth in this statement above. If you
could speed up the vibrational rate of your molecular structure

you could match it with any physical object and then, quite literally, walk through that object. But it is not like that; we are vibrating very slowly. The purpose of this is so we can learn to interact with the densest physical matter. This is the hardest thing to deal with but offers the greatest liberation. Any soul can walk through walls, or float off through space; it takes an act of great courage to manifest on a material plane like this (and all of us reading this book inevitably are in this state) to learn the experiences of denseness. Our awareness is thus expanded to include denseness of physical existence as well as the lightness of incorporeal being.

In the physical world we can experience ourselves as strong or weak. Around us we have varying degrees of both walls of strength and of weakness.

Relax and centre.

Tune in to whether you feel more in touch with 'strength' or 'weakness' at this time. Be whichever of these you are, give yourself a voice, and start to tell the other about yourself. Actually speak out loud as you do this.

Then get out of your seat, sit somewhere else in your room, and become the other one, 'strength' or 'weaknesses'. Talk back to the other part, and then, swapping seats when necessary, keep a dialogue going between these two energies.

Then get weakness to voice its strengths and strength to voice its weaknesses.

Dancing

One way to really get in touch with the physical world and express yourself physically is through dancing. Dancing does not have to be anything formal or particular. Simply choose some rhythmic music and let your body move. It can help you to get started if you concentrate on a pa..cular part of your body, then let other parts join in. Similarly, you can choose particular types of movement, and then practise putting them together. For example, you might move very jerkily and with little short steps for a while, then do some really expansive, flowing movements, then put the two together. Part of the creative spirit of dancing, and its fun too, is allowing yourself to 'become the dance', simply letting it happen without forcing anything, and without thinking about it.

Relax and centre.

Imagine you are in your meadow and take some time grounding yourself. A dancer appears from the distance and starts dancing very gracefully towards you. You watch his or her movements and style with great pleasure. When the dancer reaches you, he or she invites you to join. Start dancing with the dancer, and let yourself be inspired by the grace and beauty of his or her form. Dance together in the meadow for as long as you desire.

Then holding onto the image, return to your room and start dancing!

Massage

All the various body-orientated therapies such as bioenergetics, Heller work, the Alexander technique and so on, are ways of helping you get in touch with your physical form, release negative-holding patterns and manifest yourself in a clearer, more dynamically meaningful way. Perhaps the simplest 'body therapy' is touch. When we consciously touch another human being, we are entering into a richly rewarding interaction, a relationship based on respect and care. Of course, touch can be used negatively, too, to manipulate and control, to give vent to anger, to fulfil our own needs selfishly at the expense of the other person involved. This kind of touch is not truly conscious, however. Conscious touching inevitably involves respect, for when we are aware of our acts and tune into our feelings, we find that being given the opportunity to touch another person – or to be touched – is a truly magnificent experience.

There are many kinds of massage, the common link being that they are primarily based upon touch. While it is both exciting and very useful to learn various strokes, patterns and ways of touching through massage, we are all capable of giving a massage to another person. If you are not sure what to do but you want to massage someone, you cannot go far wrong if you trust your intuition and touch the other person in the way you like being touched yourself. If you feel uncertain about anything, you can always ask your partner what he or she likes, what parts of the body to touch, whether to touch with firmness or lightly, in long or short strokes, briefly or lingeringly. Remember, too, that you can always massage yourself – after all, no one knows what you need more than you do yourself! In modern cultures, we are all too often conditioned into not touching ourselves, as if there is something wrong with it. The next exercise involves self-massage. Before starting, you might like to think about your environment, dimming the light, lighting a candle and incense, or doing whatever creates, for you, an atmosphere of peace and calm.

Relax and centre.

Recline or lie in a comfortable place that is neither too hard nor too soft. Put your attention on to your body, and notice what areas feel tense, or uncomfortable, or 'out of tune'. Spend some time finding these areas of your body, then start massaging yourself in whatever way feels good to you right now. Spend as long or as short a time doing this as feels right. Trust your intuition, and move your hands on to other areas of your body, touching yourself in whatever way you choose.

Now tune into a place on your body where you know you enjoy being touched. Give yourself pleasure. Let yourself sink into the feeling, and continue with this until you feel ready to stop. Before moving on to anything else, lie there for a while, in your relaxed state, and feel your body's appreciation of you and your self-massage.

Sexual Energy

We gain access to and express emotions through the body. There is a great difference between experiencing an emotion, then processing it with your thoughts, and experiencing an emotion and directly expressing it with your body. Both experiences have their place, but through the direct body experience we can more readily access and, if we wish, change our emotional life.

You can only release the quantity of energy that you have built up in the first place. This is true of all aspects of energy, but particularly relevant to sexual experiences. If you are not sufficiently excited (that is, if you have not built up enough energy), however hard you try you will not reach a climax. Conversely, once you pass a certain level of excitement there is, so to speak, 'no going back' and climax becomes inevitable. It is when we 'let go' in this way that we release our energy in a full and satisfying orgasm. When the charge is high enough to get you to the peak experience, you enter spiritual or 'transpersonal' realms. In this state, you are contacting the self through your body, and realising who you really are.

The following suggestions may be used singly or in combination as aids to tuning into your awareness during sexual experiences. These can be with another person, or imaginatively adapted, on one's own. If you are with another person, remember that sharing is a great magnifier of energy.

- While in foreplay, imagine the caressing to confer everlasting life.

- Imagine your senses are open doors, and fully let in the experiences.

- Wherever your attention is drawn, go there, and at that place, experience.

- At the start of intercourse, keep attention on this moment, and avoid passing towards the end by constantly starting afresh.

- Look into your partner's face, and see him or her as if for the very first time.

- When your body starts into orgasm, become a leaf in the wind, and enter carelessly into the shaking.

- Imagine the space you both occupy as being without limit.

- After your orgasm, while you are still joined, feel waves of peace rise from the ground and envelop your bodies.

- Look into the distance, beyond your partner's gaze, and feel the serenity.

- Realise your partner as a manifestation of the god or goddess.

Your Body

Tune into that part of your body which you feel is most valuable to you. Why is it so important? What quality does it embody? Is it strength, joy, peace, truth, togetherness, balance, love or whatever? This is a soul quality in your body. All parts of your body carry such qualities.

Each of us, as individual souls, become incarnate through our bodies, and our bodies then hold and express the archetypes and qualities we have to manifest throughout our life journeys. Each part of the body is a manifestation of some part of the self. Our feet are our most densely incarnated parts, and the qualities they reveal are generally those of manifestation and strength. At the other end of our body, at the very top of the head we find more abstract qualities such as truth and light.

The next exercise can most effectively be performed outdoors, somewhere where you can walk without too much obstruction or distraction – for example, in a local park. You can try it out in your home, however.

All you have to do is just walk. This is not as simple as it sounds. When we walk we are usually involved with thinking, feeling, sensing, imagining and all the other components of our inner dialogue. You talk to yourself about where you have come from, where you are going, what you might do when you get there and so on. You make comments (hopefully subvocally!) about the people you see as you pass them by. Perhaps certain locations bring up memories for you, recent or more distant ones. None of this is 'just walking'. To do this you have first to centre yourself.

First, therefore, centre yourself in whatever way you choose. You might just simply say to yourself: 'I am I, I have thoughts, feelings, senses, but they are not me. I have them, they do not have me. I am now choosing to be centred and unattached to the contents of my consciousness. I am I.' When you feel ready, start walking, and focus on this centred awareness.

Whenever you feel yourself become identified or caught up with some distracting thought or feeling, stop, remember who you are and your choice to be centred, then start walking again. Keep this up for some time, and when you have finished note what sorts of distractions happened to you. Next time you try this exercise you can be particularly alert to these factors and avoid them more easily.

One of the problems encountered when we try to just be or just do (whether it is walking, meditating or whatever act we choose) is that there are parts within us which do not choose to simply be here. Apart from the obvious issues of being off in a fantasy, projecting and so on, which we have already discussed, there is also the state of not wanting to be incarnated, not wanting to be here on the planet. It is hard to be alive, and I would rather remain in a state of undifferentiated bliss. Why do I have to be here? Take me back home! Our fears of incarnating can hold us back from being fully present with what we do in a deeper and subtler way than simple distractions.

Look at the ways you avoid incarnation fully. Look for 'yes but. . .' responses to things you could do which would manifest you more clearly, which would bring your purpose to ground. Bronwen, for example, never quite made up her mind about anything – she wanted to leave her job and start a textile business, but. . . what if? Whenever she was faced with a decision about doing something for herself, something that would be creatively fulfilling, she avoided it – she sidetracked on the issue. In a way, she remained 'stuck in between' the two worlds of manifestation and spirit. She actually found the just walking exercise of little use, it allowed her to continue avoiding her issues. But when she started dancing, and while dancing focusing on her fears, she found a new source of energy in her body which was released through the physical exercise and made available to her.

When you are undertaking serious work on yourself, it is really advisable to eat a good diet. There are so many books on diet and healthy eating available, you might be confused and lost for choice. Are you really what you eat? Perhaps you are in a more literal sense than intended by this question, but whether you are or not, you are most certainly affected by what you eat. Notice the difference in yourself fifteen minutes after eating a hamburger and French fries compared with a plate of fresh, raw organic vegetables. You have to make your own decisions about what you are going to eat. But whatever you do decide, make the choice with consciousness and clear decision. Do not become rigid about any diet, however healthy it is, but at the same time do not allow laziness or carelessness to divert you from your chosen course. If you eat with awareness you will find yourself choosing to eat what is appropriate for you at any particular time.

We can start to heal ourselves of the fears that we carry in our bodies, fears built up either from our responses to real experiences, or those based upon imaginary happenings, which to the body are no less 'real' than those based on actual events. The following exercise helps in such healing.

Relax and centre.

Start to breathe deeply, and connect your in-breath with your out-breath. Without forcing it, make your breathing as deep as you can, and keep it going in a continuous cycle.

After a few minutes of this deep breathing, ask your body where it is holding fear. You might receive the answer in words, or you might simply experience sensations in some part of your body. Trust that your body has the wisdom to lead you to the most appropriate place for healing to occur. Put your attention on the chosen area and really connect with it. Contact the fear you are holding in this place – what does the fear look like, how does it smell, what sounds are associated with it, what does it feel like?

Ask your body what colour it needs to dissolve the fear. Accept the first colour you see, hear or feel.

Imaginatively draw that colour into your body with your in-breath and feel it filling up that area of your body until you cannot receive any more. Keep breathing in the colour until you sense that you have taken in enough.

Be aware that colour can absorb and dissolve the fear within you. Let it do just that.

When you feel ready, open your eyes and bring your consciousness back to your room. Lie quietly for a while, feeling the new space you have created through dissolving this fear.

Areas of our bodies, even the body as a whole, can become rigidified. This might be because you fear the external world, and you start holding yourself tight to avoid contact with what is out there. This might have been when you were a child, and you have unconsciously held the pattern of rigidity ever since. Or it might be the outcome of more recent events. In either case, you can only overcome this kind of rigidity through letting go of the tightness and opening up to your emotions. You may have to relive some of the painful experiences that led to the wall of rigidity being erected in the first place. But even pain of immense power experienced through this kind of cathartic work is nothing compared to the pain you can experience through rigidity.

You may have constructed a wall of rigidity from fear of the inside rather than what is outside. You might, for example, be afraid of the power you find within yourself, or you may be afraid you have nothing inside. In either case, you have to realise who you are before you can de-rigidify, and dissolve these walls. If there is 'too much' inside, realise you are a mere speck in the universe, a passing moment in time. Knowing yourself as a transitory being is humbling enough to alleviate all such fears of power. Alternatively, if you fear 'too little', then work more on yourself through meditation and visualisations, and realise how much there actually is inside you, that you are a rich storehouse of inspiration, poetic visions and life-giving energies.

· 9 ·

THE SINGLE SELF
Exploring Attachment

The world is such and such or so and so only because we talk to ourselves about its being such and such or so and so.

CARLOS CASTANEDA

Just as we looked in a previous chapter at the ways we can be attached to subpersonalities, and saw how our personality is really composed of these 'little selves', similarly we can look at these parts of our personality in terms of body, feelings and thoughts. Body, feelings and thoughts are not really separate but we can 'look through the glasses' of each. The soul has a body, has feelings and has thoughts, not the reverse. In other words, you could say that a soul has you, not that you have a soul. The orchestra does not lead the conductor, quite the opposite. The soul is not dependent upon the personality, the soul is the soul. But it has lessons to learn, experiences it chooses to have, so incarnates and comes into the world with this clothing of body, feelings and thoughts in order to have these experiences. The soul is evolving, it is in a state of process, having chosen to incarnate and live through this life to aid evolution. We can either go with this process or we can fight against it.

Figure 5 illustrates how our physical, emotional and thinking functions develop from our birth onwards. Of course, these developments do not happen independently, but each seven-year period, as illustrated in the diagram, has one of the functions foremost for development. The others are also developing, but not in the foreground. Also the seven-year divisions are approximate averages, and not meant as rigidly defined age barriers. They present an overall picture, not the exact truth for any given individual.

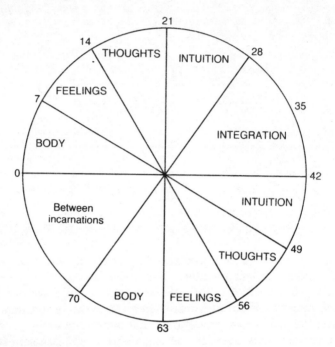

Figure 5: The Cycle of Life

As the diagram shows, uppermost for development in the 0–7 year period is the body, which clearly agrees with our knowledge of the developing child. Of course, it must be stressed that other functions are developing through this period, we are simply saying that the body is the foreground developmental issue. Then during the 7–14 period emotional development is foreground (including the onset of puberty), 14–21 intellectual development, and so on.

The diagram is also interesting when we look at the second half of life. Working backwards we can see that in the last seven years the physical becomes foreground again. Any issues not dealt with effectively in the first seven years are 'repeated' or 'brought up again' during this period. It is almost as if the soul creates a reprise, offering the individual the opportunity for further lesson learning and integration. In the last but one seven-year stage (approximating to 56–63 years) there is a repeat of the emotional development period (interestingly being the age groups where heart attacks are most likely to happen), and so on.

The diagram puts the end of life at 70, and it must be stressed this division of life into ten seven-year cycles is fairly artificial, for most people live more than seventy years anyway. It is meant to be representative of the cycles of growth and integration we go through in life rather than a rigid system. Used in this way it can be most useful. Also, as the life span for most people (in the western world anyway) increases, we may find that the period for integration (suggested on the diagram as being between 28 and 42) will increase, with the four seven-year cycles at the end of life simply moving 'later'.

Walls are built in the personality to stop the full experience of the soul. This is necessary or the soul energy would be so strong it would overwhelm or 'blow out' the personality. The problem lies in the fact that other walls are built which do not further our growth but rather hinder it. This leads us to ask ourselves the question: What in our personality blocks us from being more fully ourselves? There can be no doubt that self actualisation is a life-time process. We need to align our personalities with soul, the manifestor of the self, then we are able to follow the next step to whatever is necessary for our development.

We will look in detail at the various kinds of resistance to the self that we can develop. For now, see how you have the choice to partner soul or not, and try to discriminate and to trust the process of unfoldment. If you resist, what gets energised is the resistance, and this resistance will then continue until a crisis happens. You can work on resistances at any stage, but like all things you will find them easier to deal with when they are still small. You are better off dealing with resistances sooner rather than later.

Watch for illuminations, inspirations, dreams, synchronicities and visions that emerge into your consciousness. Do not expect these special moments, but also watch that you do not miss them.

Developing Your Functions

For a full, holistic development of your personality it is important to build your relationship with your thinking, feeling and sensing functions. This relationship is primarily developed through differentiation. When something is happening, when you are experiencing or expressing something – anything – stop and ask yourself: What is this? Is this sensing, feeling or thinking? This will help you get a clearer picture of which of these functions are less developed in your personality, offering you the opportunity to raise the energy of these underdeveloped parts, mainly through inclusion. You can also work on functions which have become repressed, and allow more balance where it is needed, thus enabling you to experience sensing, feeling and thinking in a less extreme way. Each function must be made whole before it can be synthesised with other functions and fully brought into an integrated personality.

Part of your task with this work is to find ways to use the environment to support your work, rather than going against it. If you are currently working on developing a more balanced relationship with your emotional function, for example, is it appropriate for you to go to that wild party tonight (it may be)? If your mental function needs development, is a comic book the best reading material?

You can then purify and raise the level of each function to a higher vibration, continuously refining, so each function – body, feelings and mind – can become a clear channel for the expression of the soul. Ask yourself questions like: What are the soul qualities trying to come through at this time? How can I evoke and develop these desired qualities? Would this be a good time to seek inner guidance? Shall I meditate on this now so that I am more aligned with my inner purpose?

It is also important to look at the relationship between sensing, feeling and thinking, asking yourself how well do they work together in my personality? Then when problems arise, you can see them as opportunities to find out more about what is happening underneath, what is behind the problem. You can then work on this deeper level.

You can look at the relationship between these functions by, for instance:

- 'time sharing' (giving all the functions space for expression in your daily life); for example, if you give an angry emotional part of you space for expression, perhaps by channelling the aggression into some physically exhausting work, it will then not come up inappropriately at other times, but will more readily 'time share' with other parts of your personality.

• 'dialoguing' (allowing different functions to communicate with one another to see what each has to say, both in terms of what it needs but also what it can give); you could, for example, resolve a conflict between an emotional subpersonality that wants you to stay at home and an intellectual subpersonality that wants you to go to an important but anxiety-ridden meeting through allowing them to talk to one another and come to some agreement, even if it is only temporary. You can do what is needed through listening to the voice of both these parts.

• 'reconciliating' (finding ways of bringing together parts of these functions that feel antagonistic to each other because of past experience); for example, perhaps two parts of your personality agreed to some 'time sharing' and one part reneged on the deal. Before the part who feels betrayed will be willing to come to any further agreement, you will have to reconcile what happened and try to find ways to overcome the lack of trust involved in this.

• 'fantasising' (asking yourself questions such as: What would it be like if. . . were working together?) The more you are able to visualise the results of different parts of yourself working together, the more they will be able to do just that. If you cannot imagine it then it is so much less likely to happen.

You may be surprised to find out how wise you are when you discover effective ways of following these techniques. Trust in yourself as a soul, and allow inner wisdom to bring your vehicles for expression into a more harmonious relationship.

As with all growth work, the final test is how well you can express all this in your daily life. To be truly spiritual and connected is not to be off somewhere having a trip, however spiritually blissful it may be. It is to be here, right now, in whatever you are doing. Hopefully, when you are able to do this, you will find it the most spiritually blissful trip of all. You are part of a greater whole, you have chosen to be here, to manifest in life, you have unlimited potential, and you have already chosen the basic pattern of your life. When you trust in yourself in this way, you can use your will and your awareness to enhance not only your personal evolution, but through you, the evolution of the planet as a whole.

We are most creative when we are alone. When we are alone we are 'all one'. Meditate on this, for it expresses a positive truth. To be creative within, and then to manifest this creativity, you need first to disidentify from the parts (the body, the feelings and the thoughts) and then identify with the self as you experience it as an individual soul.

Self-Identification

The experience of self-identification, of having an 'I', distinguishes our consciousness from that of the majority of other sentient beings on our planet. This self-consciousness, however, is usually experienced, not as *pure* self-consciousness, but rather mixed with and veiled by the *contents* of consciousness, that is, everything we are sensing, feeling and/or thinking at any time. We usually live our lives *identified with* these contents of our consciousness. To make self-consciousness an explicit, experiential fact in our lives we need first to dis-identify from the 'contents' of consciousness.

Most people tend to be generally more attached to either their thoughts or their emotions, and can thus be described as mentally or emotionally identified. Such identification can be useful at times, even necessary, but to live a balanced life we need to cultivate the sphere in which we are deficient as well as be able to dis-identify from all these spheres of experience and expression. Thus people who are predominantly identified with their thoughts, who are, in other words, mentally identified, need to increase their awareness, experience and expression of their feelings, rather than diminish or decrease their mental awareness. If we picture the situation as one where mind and feelings are unequally developed, and therefore of unequal size, the technique is to increase the size of the smaller one so that it matches the size of the larger one. This is balance through upward growth and increase, rather than through decrease, which is both unnecessary and inefficient.

Through deliberate dis-identification from the personality and identification with the self, we gain freedom, and the power to choose either attachment to or dis-attachment from any aspect of our personality, according to what is most appropriate for any given situation. Thus we may learn to utilise our whole personality in an inclusive and harmonious synthesis.

The following exercise is a tool for moving towards and realising the consciousness of the self. This exercise, called 'Self Identification', is central to the theme of this book, and should be done with the greatest care. If you feel at all tired do not read on from here until you have at least taken a break. You will enjoy this exercise more if you are fresh when you first try it out.

Relax and centre.

Follow these instructions slowly and carefully.

Affirm to yourself the following:

'I have a body, but I am not my body. My body may find itself in different conditions of health or sickness, it may be rested or tired, but that has nothing to do with my self, my real I. I value my body as my precious instrument of experience and action in the world, but it is only an instrument. I treat it well, I seek to keep it in good health, but it is not myself. *I have a body, but I am not my body.*'

Close your eyes, recall what this affirmation says, then focus your attention on the central concept: 'I have a body, but I am not my body'.

Attempt to realise this as an experienced fact in your consciousness.

Now proceed with the following two affirmations, treating them in the same way, realising the central affirmation in each as an experienced fact.

'I have emotions, but I am not my emotions. My emotions are diversified, changing, sometimes contradictory. They may swing from love to hatred, from calm to anger, from joy to sorrow, and yet my essence – my true nature – does not change. I remain. Though a wave of anger may temporarily submerge me, I know that in time it will pass; therefore I am not this anger. Since I can observe and understand my emotions, and can gradually learn to direct, utilise, and integrate them harmoniously, it is clear that they are not my self. *I have emotions, but I am not my emotions.'*

'I have a mind, but I am not my mind. My mind is a valuable tool of discovery and expression, but it is not the essence of my being. Its contents are constantly changing as it embraces new ideas, knowledge and experience, and makes new connections. Sometimes it seems to refuse to obey me. Therefore it cannot be me, my self. It is an organ of knowledge in regard to both the outer and inner worlds, but it is not my self. *I have a mind, but I am not my mind.'*

Next comes the phase of identification. Affirm clearly and slowly to yourself:

'After this dis-identification of my self, the I, from the contents of consciousness, emotions, sensations, thoughts, I recognise and affirm that I am a centre of pure self-consciousness. I am a centre of will, capable of observing, directing and using all my psychological processes and my physical body.'

Focus your attention on the central realisation:

'I am a centre of pure self-consciousness and of will.'

Realise this as an *experienced* fact in your awareness.

When you have practised this exercise a few times, you can use it in a much shorter form. You can personalise it, too, if you wish, so long as you keep to the four main, central affirmations:

I have a body and sensations, but I am not my body and sensations.

I have feelings and emotions, but I am not my feelings and emotions.
I have a mind and thoughts, but I am not my mind and thoughts.
I am I, a centre of pure self-consciousness and of will.

You may have to repeat the exercise a few times to start with to get the full flavour, but then you will be able to do it daily from memory. The effort will be well worth it. This exercise is effective if practised daily, preferably during the first few hours of the day. It can then be considered as a second, symbolic reawakening.

It is often thoughts that are the hardest from which to dis-identify. We construct our world through our thoughts about it, and so it is apparent that when we stop thinking about our world its basic structures tumble. Walls created from thought have an apparent permanence and we can deeply fear their dissolution. When we stop this internal thinking, this inner dialogue with ourselves, special and extraordinary aspects of ourselves surface, as though they have previously been heavily walled to protect us from their power and truth. If you stop the internal dialogue you create the inner space – aloneness or 'all one-ness' – to be able to tune into what you want to happen in your life, what your true purpose is, and then to find ways to make it happen.

Janet was mentally identified; when she thought of anything she always thought of its opposite, so like a snake with a tail in its mouth, she needed to stop sucking her tail to break the cycle. But whenever that happened it always popped back in. Then, at a late stage of the work, in a visualisation, she chose to bite the tail off (rid herself of the identification) which she did through sharpening her teeth (doing dis-identification work). Now she can suck the tail or not suck it as she chooses. Once she took the courage to do it, and bit the tail off, she found it was still there, available to her when wanted, but no longer as an attachment.

When we dis-identify we can then choose to re-identify. That is the goal. We do not want to be without our vehicles for expression and experience, we want to have them rather than them having us. Tony had a very profound experience during dis-identification. In his own words: 'I've got an image of a funnel, I'm a cone resting on my point and I sway around but the point is firmly fixed. I'm a trumpet, a horn, sometimes I am blown too loudly and sometimes I don't make a sound at all. I'm just an instrument, it's how I'm played that makes me appear different. I can be played to make nice music or horrible rasping sounds. Sometimes I like to be played on my own, sometimes with the orchestra, sometimes I don't get blown and sometimes I get blown inappropriately. What I need is just to be allowed. Try blowing me different ways, you don't have to always push with all your breath, breathe with me, breathe in and out with me, I can make sounds whether you are breathing in or out. I need to be used more harmoniously with the other instruments, use me and blow me, but be aware of the other parts of you as well.'

The following exercise involves a dialogue between the soul and the personality.

Relax and centre.

Sit on a chair or cushion with a second chair or cushion conveniently placed in front of you, facing in your direction. Imagine that your soul sits on that chair. Without trying too hard, engage your soul in a dialogue. Start by telling it something about what you think, feel or sense.

When you feel ready, move positions, sit on the chair or cushion opposite and become your soul. Look back at yourself as a personality in the original position, and answer back. Say whatever comes to you.

At your own pace, allow a dialogue to happen between your personality and your soul. Do not try to make it anything special, or force it in any way, but simply see what happens. And watch for non-verbal messages that might come from the soul chair, such as particular body postures, facial expressions, gestures and so on.

You can use this exercise to bring greater understanding between you and soul, and also to find inner guidance on issues of importance to you. You have to separate the medium from the message. What your soul tells you will be the truth, but the way you hear the message can be distorted. Be careful not to expect the advice to be too concrete, it usually is not, but it should be supportive in at least the long term. It is also important to discriminate, to look for non-verbal reinforcement, any changes in body position or breath patterns that suggest whether the dialogue is working effectively. Also watch for judgements creeping in – the soul is never judgemental towards the personality – firm yes, but angry no.

Try to find ways to express in your daily life what the soul tells you so you can check its validity in the real world. Remember you are the soul and you have a personality, not vice versa. Do not worry if the exercise does not work too well for you – it certainly does not mean you are without a soul. It might be simply that the exercise is not right for you in some way, or it might be that, at this time in your personal evolution, your soul is choosing to work 'undercover' and a dialogue would be inappropriate. Trust that your own process is unfolding as it is meant to and you cannot go far wrong.

The following table illustrates some of the important qualitative differences between the realms of the soul and the personality and is useful both to help distinguish the qualities of each but also to check the validity of messages you receive from the soul.

QUALITIES OF THE TWO REALMS

Soul Realm	Personality Realm
universality	individuality
urge to share	attached to desire
will and purpose	satisfaction of desires
solidarity with others¹	interest in self
timeless	dependent upon time
global view	linear view
sense of abundance	fear of scarcity
quality oriented	event oriented

These two realms are not really separate; it is an illusion created by the personality, or parts of the personality, that makes us believe so. The personality is necessary to bring the soul into form, to manifest it on the planet, to experience life and learn the lessons necessary for its evolution. We have to learn to cherish our personalities, and their physical, emotional and mental functions, in the same way we cherish our planet which gives us the material base, the opportunity for our evolution.

· 10 ·

FREEDOM TO CHOOSE
Exploring Awareness and Power

You are never given a wish without also being given the power to make it true. You may have to work for it, however.

RICHARD BACH

Wherever you are and whatever you are doing, although you may not be conscious of it at that time, you have chosen to be in that place, doing that act. At this moment you are choosing to be reading these words. If this was not true you would be doing something else, something else you were choosing to do. Yet how conscious are you of your choice? Why did you pick this book up and start reading Chapter 10? There could be a variety of reasons, not necessarily exclusive: for example,

- you have read the previous nine chapters and are enjoying the book;
- you have read the previous nine chapters, are not enjoying the experience, but do not want to stop reading for one reason or another;
- you have picked the book up and have randomly opened at this page;
- you have read the book before and are looking up exercises on developing the will;
- and so on.

But how conscious were you in your choice to read this? Did you clearly and consciously choose this right now? If you did, read on; if not, make a clear decision right now either to read this or not, and then abide by your choice.

A lot of the time, to varying degrees, it seems to us as if we are not really choosing, we are drifting or muddling along waiting for the next moment when we can make a conscious choice. At these times we act like victims – victims of circumstance, of where we are or who we are, of poverty or depression, of failure or even success! It is as if we have arrived at our current situation through a series of accidents. We have made some choices along the way, but many of those have not really been effective. We have not been free to choose what we clearly and precisely want, and to know we will then get our wish fulfilled. We have been told since we were children we need to face the 'reality' of life. We cannot have everything we want.

We cannot have everything we want. Perhaps this is true, perhaps not, but how can we ever find out if we do not have freedom to choose, if we do not even know how to choose clearly? The purpose of this chapter is to give you information and assist your understanding through exercises, of both how to find out what it is you want to choose and to help you learn to choose more clearly.

For the following exercise you will need two sheets of A4 paper and a pen.

Relax and centre.

Make a list of things you want. Start each time with 'I want. . .' and simply list what it is you do want. Do ~~you~~ not judge or censor your list, include everything you can think of, including both spiritual and personal desires.

For example, this is part of a list produced by Jane:

'I want freedom
I want a new car
I want to be hugged
I want love
I want the truth
I want to run away
I want lots of money
I want a new dress
I want a whole new wardrobe
I want to know myself better
I want a gooey cake. . .'

Do not stop until you have at least twenty 'wants', and continue for longer if you wish.

When you have finished, look at this list and deliberate over your choices. Underline those that seem the most important, then deliberate some more and double underline those of prime importance. Really affirm that these are the most important desires you currently have.

When you have done this decide on the one 'I want. . .' which you believe to be, at this very moment, the one of greatest concern to you. Decide clearly on one choice.

Turn your paper over and write this one 'I want. . .' in large letters. As you write it, strongly affirm that this is currently your most overriding choice. Do not underestimate the importance of constantly affirming, and, if necessary, reaffirming your intention. Affirmation reinforces the will.

We will now do some reflective meditation on this choice. Take your second piece of paper and put a circle in the middle with your 'I want. . .' written in it. Contemplate the ways you could achieve this goal. Put each possibility on a ray coming out from the circle. Continue this contemplation until you have several alternative ways of achieving your desire. Again, at this stage, do not censor or judge your responses.

Jane chose her wish for a new car as her most overriding desire, and her meditation ended up looking like this:

Figure 6: The 'Wants' Meditation

127

Through this meditation you have been planning how you could manifest or concretise your desire. It makes no difference at this stage whether you chose something more abstract such as the desire for 'Truth' or something concrete such as the desire for a new car, you will now know several ways in which you could at least move closer to that goal if not necessarily fully achieve it.

The final stage in this exercise is the execution of your desire. You have to do it. From your planning you have several choices, some of which may be more immediately practical than other ways. For example, in Jane's planning for a new car she can more easily save £20 a month than she can choose to win the football pools. She can, however, start doing the pools, to at least have a chance! Be creative in how you interpret these plans, and execute as many of them as you can. See if you can start realising this desire, and repeat the process for other desires. You will find you are freer to choose than you previously imagined.

In the last exercise you actually went through six stages:

1.   Investigation (making a list of your wants to find out what it is you desire).

2.   Deliberation (over the wants to select the currently more relevant ones).

3.   Decision (upon the one want you wish to work with, that is most important to you at the present time).

4.   Affirmation (that this one want is the most important, by writing it out again and starting to concretise it, through constantly reaffirming your attention).

5.   Plan (doing reflective meditation, and thinking about how you could actually concretise this desire, how you could make it happen).

6.   Execution (doing it, finding ways of carrying out your plans, either in entirety or step by step).

Every choice you make involves these six stages to a greater or lesser degree. It might be that for a particular choice you know what you want, hardly deliberate over it at all, and are able quickly to plan and execute the action necessary to succeed in manifesting your will – for example, your walk to a nearby park this afternoon.

On the other hand, you might find it hard to know what you want, and you might endlessly deliberate over the choices and never actually decide what to do. Or you might decide and not be sure how to go about planning and executing the necessary actions. Or it might be something well worked out but for which the execution needs to take place at a particular time. If you choose a sunset you will be able to make it happen, but only at the right time of day! Your choice has to conform to natural laws or it is doomed to failure.

We have to remember that our choices are global – in two senses. Firstly, while they surely include all the six stages, they rarely do so in linear fashion. It is not a simple 1 through 6 and hey presto! For instance, while planning you may need to go back and deliberate further when you discover that you have not quite got the choice right. Often you need to keep going back to your choice to affirm it over and over. Constantly returning to the affirmation stage to focus on and strengthen your choice is a well-known technique. It will reinforce the planning and execution of your will.

Our choices are global in a second way, too. Every choice we make affects everything and everyone else. On a very simple level, if you choose to eat this particular apple right at this moment no one else can eat it either now or at any other time. On a more complex – and perhaps deeply meaningful level – if you choose to ignore an injustice of which you are aware, while it may go unnoticed or uncorrected for some time, the situation will only worsen. Little things invariably grow into larger things. We blithely ignore the starving millions in our global village until the situation reaches crisis point, then we act upon this with short-term solutions.

Everything we choose to do affects someone or something else in some way. We must make our choices clearly and with heart, and be aware of this global effect, yet we must not allow such knowledge to make us impotent. Rather we must try to align ourselves with the flow of nature so that our choices add to rather than subtract from the evolution of consciousness on our planet.

If I ask you to do something right now, what choices are

available to you? Think about your answer to this question before continuing.

So if I now ask you to raise your right arm in the air, what are the choices you have?

Or what if I ask you to kill someone?

The two obvious choices are yes and no, I will and I will not. We often miss, however, the third choice which is usually available to us – 'not for now'. Sometimes it is right to make a speedy decision. The question at hand needs a fast response, or the choice you are making seems obvious. There is nothing wrong with fast, hasty decisions when appropriate. But often we would do well to consider our choices. Perhaps we are unable to make what is an informed decision immediately. Perhaps it is something we cannot do yet, but might be able to do in the future.

Do not limit yourself by saying yes or no when 'not for now' is more appropriate. Keep your options open where possible. If I ask you to make a sunset appear, what is your response? If I ask you, right now, physically to walk through a closed door, what will you choose?

Freedom

There are two kinds of freedom, freedom from and freedom for. These are well illustrated by examples, as shown in the following table.

Freedom from	Freedom for
conditioning	pursuit of positive goals
the past	the future
external authority	manifestation of positive interests
patterns of reaction	manifesting real preferences
compulsive behaviour	learning to be free
the need to escape	courage
dependency on others	autonomy
involuntary acts	spontaneity
self-denial	self-acceptance

Freedom *from* allows us to deal with the past, all our conditioning and learning, and make decisions in the present moment, not unconnected to our previous knowledge and learning but not blindly controlled by these factors.

Freedom *for* allows us to see into the future and connect with our potential, to make decisions in the present moment with a clear insight into how our potential may manifest.

We need *both* freedom from and freedom for.

In a sense we all accept the conditioning that some things are 'sinful'. This concept of 'sin' is something we need freedom *from*. The word is derived from a Greek word which meant 'missing the mark'. In other words, the only true sin is to miss the mark, that is to deviate from our true, inner function or Purpose. This 'Purpose' has also been called the True Will. As we learn to connect more deeply with our inner purpose we begin to get a sense of this True Will as the deepest, most spiritual and yet most manifest sense of our Purpose for being incarnated. True Will manifests itself in steps which can take towards its unfoldment. It is a distant goal, yet each conscious step we take is on the path towards its fruition.

The most important use of freedom *for* is for the manifestation of this True Will. The more freedom to choose we acquire, the more we find ourselves doing just that, feeling sufficiently free to be able to make positive, life-enhancing choices that manifest our inner purpose and guidance.

For the following exercise, called 'The Purpose Visualisation'. You will need one sheet of A4 paper and a pen. You might like to use colours also.

Relax and centre.

Either choose your 'I want' from the previous exercise, or select one of the other desires you arrived at in that exercise. Or alternatively you could do the exercise again. Whichever you choose, find for yourself which desire is the strongest in you at this present moment.

Write this desire at the top of your paper.

Close your eyes and say the desire over to yourself several times: 'I want [whatever it is]'. As you say this, allow a symbol or image for this desire to emerge in your consciousness. Do not force it, just let the image appear.

And do not censor it; whatever emerges is the right image for you at this moment.

For example, Jane, when doing this exercise, chose her desire for 'love'. An obvious symbol she might have imagined would have been a glowing red heart. Instead the symbol that emerged was a blue triangle! She chose that as her symbol for her desire for love.

Draw a simple representation of your image or symbol on your piece of paper, colouring it appropriately if you so desire.

Close your eyes and imagine you are standing on top of a hill. Stretching before you is a perfectly straight road that slopes down into and crosses a valley, then climbs up a hill that you can see in the distance. At the end of the road, at the top of the distant hill, you can see a large sign that incorporates your symbol.

Start walking down the road, taking your time but not deviating at all from the straight road that leads through the valley and up the other hill. Be aware of any distractions that occur, whether they be, for example, a beautiful flower that beckons you to stop and look at it or a demonic figure that tries to pull you from the path. Be aware of these distractions but do not follow them. Keep to the road, walking with determination towards your goal at the top of the far hill.

As you climb the distant hill, look ahead and see your image, your symbol, getting larger and larger as you get closer to it. Keep walking up the hill until you reach the top, by which time your symbol has assumed gigantic proportions. When you arrive in front of it make a clear affirmation of your desire, for example: 'This is my desire to have love'. Allow the energy of the symbol to infuse through your whole body, to penetrate into your feelings and to fill your thoughts.

Become the symbol.

When you are ready, open your eyes and write about your experience. Make a note of the distractions from the path as well as how you felt when you reached your goal.

This exercise can be performed over and over, either with the same desire symbol or with others as they become uppermost. It helps direct your consciousness towards your desire, and helps your dream come true. And sometimes the symbol can even be transformed along the way: when Jane merged with her blue triangle, she found the heart she was looking for shining brightly at its centre.

A week or so after performing this exercise for the first time, check for results. Have you succeeded in manifesting your desire, or at least in moving closer towards it? If not, what went wrong, what got in the way? See if you can find ways to overcome these problems, perhaps by making the choice more clearly, perhaps through making clear, consistent affirmations, perhaps through more detailed planning. Your success will be directly proportional to the amount of effort you are willing to put into achieving that success.

The Evolution of the Will

There are four stages in the evolution of the will in the individual; from 'having no will' (victim consciousness), through 'having a will', to 'becoming the will'. A distinction needs to be made between 'True Will' – the will of the Self, what you 'really want to do at your innermost core level' – and the energies, such as drives and self-centred desires, that come from subpersonalities. Of course, this is not to say that subpersonalities should not get what they want, their needs have to be met fully before they can truly be transformed. But their wishes are inevitably in conflict with the wishes of other subpersonalities. You experience no such conflicts with the True Will. In the following sections, exercises are presented to help the natural evolution of the will, and for developing both the strong and skilful will.

The evolution of the will, as described, is a process that can be applied to the individual as a whole and to each subpersonality.

When you have become familiar with these stages, you will find it useful to apply this 'map' to each of your subpersonalities as appropriate. To know where you are helps you to both find out where you need to go and to start moving in that direction.

STAGE 1: NO WILL/VICTIM CONSCIOUSNESS

While we are not victims and have inside us a wealth of wisdom which can guide us in any decision, it is a common human experience to feel like a victim to outside forces, other people or the circumstances in which we find ourselves. At many times in our lives we all experience a sense of impotency. 'I can't. . .' can then become all too familiar a plea. We are reactive to our environment, as if what we are and, even more importantly, what we are able to do (or not do) is totally dependent upon what happens outside of us. In such states we can be like a victim, whether to our repressed urges and desires, to basic drives, or to people or events outside of us. When we live at this level, desire is the primary motivation in our lives. There is no experience of 'being source or cause'. Our orientation is towards getting our desire(s) met and avoiding as much pain as possible along the way.

A typical day for Lyn was get up, do, do, do, go to bed. She evaluated her day by how much she could do in it and she would get stomach pains if she dared stop doing. To make things worse, she rarely if ever did enough, so she was always judging herself negatively. Doing anything to fill the time was of greatest importance and completely managed to obscure any sense of self that might emerge. She could not imagine not doing – if she tried it she would become bored and/or irritated and/or weepy. Then her stomach would start cramping and she would get on the endless roundabout of doing once more. She was a victim to this complex set of drives. She had 'no will of her own', she could never do 'just what she wanted'.

A 'victim' will often use some form of manipulation in order to get sympathy, love and attention. Unfortunately, certainly in the long term, this does not work because it keeps us smaller, or less than the one who gives the sympathy. It also reduces responsibility, so makes being a victim easier.

Say to yourself several times over: 'There's no justice in the world'. How does this fit? Do you recognise there are times when you feel like this? Are there parts of you that would agree?

In reality, however horrible the situation you are in may truly be, you can make of it what you will. You could be unjustly imprisoned and, as a victim, spend your days bemoaning your fate. You might plot revenge on those who unjustly imprisoned you, those to whom you are a victim. Or you could undertake some other plan of action – you could meditate, write, use the time to make detailed observations of yourself or your fellow inmates, and so on. There are many stories of people doing just this. Assagioli, the founder of psychosynthesis, when imprisoned by Mussolini, spent his days developing and 'fine-tuning' his system of psychology. When he was released he was that much richer for the experience. On the other hand, I doubt if he recommended it.

A victim is powerless, whereas in reality there are always two options: to be a victim or to take responsibility. One simple technique for taking responsibility is to repeat to yourself the mantra: 'I am creating this. . .' and apply it to whatever is happening to you. (Of course, even our language can imply victim consciousness – nothing is ever really 'happening *to* you' when you are creating your world afresh each moment.)

STAGE 2: UNDERSTANDING THERE IS A WILL

This understanding, that there is a will, that will does exist, comes when we realise we have a choice for any situation – yes, no or not for now. Of course, an individual may have reached this stage with some parts of the personality, and be more or less developed with other parts. But when this is experienced, however partially, there is a shift in awareness from 'I desire. . .' to 'I will. . .' In other words, there is a move from the level of wants (which tend to be inflexible – I want a blue car with red trim and nothing else will do) to the level of needs, which are usually more flexible (for example I need a new car, any colour will do so long as it works better than the existing one).

This shift also involves the development of both strong will and skilful will. Strong will is the energy to choose, skilful will the knowledge of how to use that energy. For example, the strong will is like a car, the skilful will the driver. At this stage the individual is still separate, but there is a beginning of responsibility, the knowledge that some choice is possible. There is the beginning of independence, and the development of personal power.

Make a list of things you think you should do. Start each item on your list with these words: 'I should. . .' (for example, brush my teeth every day, be a good boy, do the washing up, take charge of my own growth). When you have at least ten – and preferably more – items, go through them and, saying them out loud to yourself, see what associations or memories or states they might engender within you.

Now go through the list again but this time say them out loud clearly with the 'should' changed to a 'could' (for example, I could brush my teeth, etc.)

Answer this question: What makes an act of will successful? Think of times in your life when you have successfully willed something, that is, wanted something, made a choice to get it, and succeeded. Then think of times when you have been unsuccessful in using your will. What are the differences between these experiences?

STAGE 3: HAVING A WILL

When this stage or level is attained, it can be experienced consciously or unconsciously, and it happens, usually, as a gradual awakening. You start to become the conductor of your orchestra more often, and control which players are active and which not. When you are 'playing an instrument' you hold both an awareness of the conductor, and the ability to switch into that role when it is appropriate. There is a distinct move here towards integration of the orchestra, towards, in other words, an integrated personality. There is less fragmentation and more clarity of choice. You have a will and you can choose with it. Spiritual power is available to you as, by becoming the conductor more often, you receive 'the music' more directly from the composer. This connects you to your 'purpose', the meaning you have in your life, why you are incarnated on this planet at this time. And you have consciousness of the consequences of your actions, both those you make consciously and with choice and those you make from identified places, without consciousness. Of course, you are not conscious all of the time, but the 'percentage' is on the up.

Get four A4 or larger sheets of paper and some drawing tools (a pencil will do, colours will add to your experience).

Relax and centre.

Sit quietly and contemplate your responses to the statement: 'What I believe I am'. Reflect upon your answers, then let an image emerge in your consciousness that represents this. Do not try to judge it or censor it, just allow whatever comes. It might be an abstract symbol or it might be a person, or the detailed representation of a place. Allow the image to appear, then, when you feel ready, draw the image on your paper.

When you have finished this drawing, turn that page over and do the same for the following three statements:

- 'what I should be';
- 'what I could be';
- 'what I can become'.

STAGE 4: BEING WILL

When this stage is reached there is alignment with 'Spiritual Will', a true and deep identification with the Self. Here we are aligning ourselves with 'higher' or inner energies, contacting and becoming the composer. You can reach this level of consciousness through meditation, silence, going inside and allowing this energy of the Self to permeate through you.

Relax and centre.

Sit comfortably, breathe deeply and imagine you are in your meadow. You are going to ground yourself there by paying attention to what you sense around you – what you see, what you hear, smell, taste and can touch. Really feel the ground under your feet. When you are ready start towards the corner of your meadow from where a path leads up a nearby mountain. Taking your time, climb to the top of this mountain and find there a beautiful, serene 'Temple of Silence'. Go inside and experience this energy as fully and as openly as you are able.

When you are ready, return to your meadow, then to your ordinary waking consciousness, and bring as much of this energy with you as you can. How can you express this energy in your life? How can you, as a conductor, express this music through your orchestra?

You can learn to develop both strong and skilful will. Strong will is actual energy to do something. Skilful will is the ability to direct this energy in an appropriate way. Both strong and skilful will need to be developed for the full functioning of your ability to choose. In most people one will be developed more than the other, but there is usually room for improvement in both.

To develop strong will you can:

- do selective reading, choosing to read books – either fiction or non-fiction – that encourage this, stories of great heroic deeds against all odds, books about 'getting what you want' and so on;

- perform useless will exercises; for example, taking all the matches out of a matchbox, counting them carefully and deliberately, one by one, as you do so, then reversing the procedure. This is comparable to the exercises an athlete might perform, in themselves of no value, but all part of strengthening the ability to perform when required;

- find ways in your daily life of being strong willed; for example, if, like me, you hate washing up you can choose to do it regularly and with positive attention;

- score successes and failures; keep a score card of your acts of will, those that come off and those that do not and strive to improve your performance and score;

- make each physical act an act of will; a tall order, but you could, say, when gardening, do it consciously, bringing awareness to your acts. Or perhaps choose to do exercise, or dancing, and be aware that all your movements happen because you choose to make them happen;

You can easily devise other techniques for strengthening the strong will, but above all perform all these techniques playfully, cheerfully and with interest.

To develop skilful will you can:

- choose to be skilful in daily life; for example, when washing up ask yourself what is the most skilful way to do this, to make it most efficient and with the least expenditure of unnecessary energy? Should you wash the greasy pans or the glasses first? The development of skill is accomplished not only through what you actually do but through the attitude you have to the act being performed. It is not what you do, it is how you do it.

- be aware of how much you put into doing something, making it a conscious choice. If you put in too little energy, it is like using a spoon to move a mountain; using too much energy, like taking a forklift truck to an egg!

- most importantly do self-identification exercises and create a strong contact with your 'I', your centre of consciousness, and take decisions from this centred place. The greatest skill is making the most appropriate choices, and you can do this most effectively when you are not identified.

Part of the skill in using your will is being able to sustain the effort, not just to blow it all out in one go. Andy had trouble sustaining his will. When he went up a mountain to visit his angel he was given a golden sword. Upon bringing it back to the meadow, he found the edge had dulled and it had lost its shine. The only way to make it sharp and bright again appeared to be going back up the mountain, or to be constantly polishing it to the detriment of everything else. He found, for him, the best way of sustaining his will was to be making conscious choices as often as possible, even about 'silly little things'.

The Good Will

As well as strong and skilful will, there is also something called 'the good will'.

> *Just as a screen of a few millimeters can block the most intense solar light which has travelled millions of miles; just as a piece of porcelain insulates an electrical current strong enough to activate hundreds of motors. . . so a small psychic insulator – a lack of warmth, of sympathy and love, can block the expression of immense treasures of feelings and intelligence.*

ROBERTO ASSAGIOLI

The good will has been described as a synthesis of Love and Will, a dynamic and Joy-filled process that brings understanding and co-operation. The good will involves the recognition of the greater whole and 'right human relations'. This is basically only doing to others what you would have them do to you, and not interfering with the right of others to do as they will, so long as this does not interfere with someone else doing what they will. It is love in action.

The good will is dynamic and active; it is not just being soft and nice. It is flowing, with direction, swimming with the current, rather than against it. Sometimes called joyful will, it involves full co-operation, understanding and true empathy.

Relax and centre.

Imagine what you would be like if you had no good will at all. Maybe you would have difficulty in expressing love, you would take actions that promoted your interests at the expense of others, you might be suspicious and defensive, judgemental, prejudiced, indifferent to the suffering of others, isolated and so on. Really picture yourself as having no good will.

Now stand up and, playing the game of statues, take on the posture you would have as a person with no good will. Be really nasty! Allow yourself to be this statue, then make any movements, gestures and so on that seem appropriate. You might, for example, want to put two fingers up at the world!

Next imagine what you would be like if you had too much good will; perhaps people would walk all over you; perhaps, like a cushion, you would hold the impression of the last person who 'sat on you'. You might be overly helpful to the point of interference, unable to say no, so nice you are really sickly. Really picture yourself as having too much good will, then once again stand up and play statues with this state.

Finally imagine yourself as having just the right amount of good will, so you are truly balanced with both Love and Will, so you are co-operative and helpful and exhibit all the qualities of 'right human relations'. Stand up and start being this, but this time do not play statues, be it! Continue it for the rest of your life, each time you go away from it, coming back to it, centring again and becoming good will in this true, balanced fashion.

Purpose

Our True Will or Purpose unfolds through the individual steps we take towards its manifestation. That may seem obvious, but too often we forget this and, instead of following our path a step at a time, we try to leap ahead, not paying attention to what is happening right now. The next step is always of utmost importance, and, in actuality, the only step you can take. It is easier to stay on your path if you pay attention to your immediate position, rather than worrying about something way ahead.

Spend some time now connecting to your True Will or Purpose. You probably have some idea of what this is from the work you have already done, but for now try first reflecting upon what Purpose means to you, what you would like to manifest in your life that has 'real meaning', that is not 'ephemeral' or 'transitory', something you can do that makes a mark. Remember that Purpose is always precise, even if you do not fully understand its precision. And Purpose always follows the rule of non-interference – it cannot be your real Purpose if it involves you interfering with or altering someone else's Purpose. Take care here – it is easy to slip into interference quite unconsciously, but it is also quite easy to miss chances and become actionless through fear of interference. A fine line has to be drawn, and your balancing act well performed!

When you have connected to your Purpose – through reflection as suggested above, or through any other methods you know, which might include meditation, for example, the next step is to decide how to manifest this Purpose. Ann knew her Purpose was to serve through some kind of bodywork, perhaps massage. She had a massage qualification and for a while thought she would like to offer individual sessions of relaxing massage. She worked out the steps towards this goal and took them one at a time, paying attention along the way to any changes that might occur which would change her direction or purpose. She was, in fact, very successful until one day, about three years after having been working as a masseuse, she realised that part of her Purpose that had been hidden to her before was to do more 'hands off' work, dealing with people's energy fields rather than through direct 'hands on' massage. She reformulated her programme accordingly, which involved finding new training courses, and taking many leaps in her self-awareness. Through listening to her inner guidance, taking a step at a time, she is unfolding her Purpose in a meaningful and useful way.

It is so important, if at first you do not succeed, to try, try again. It is equally important to realise that sometimes you have got it wrong and need to change your tack in order successfully to manifest your Purpose. Finally, it cannot be overemphasised how important it is to follow through – you cannot expect things to happen immediately, all at once, 'by magic'. Real magick always works, but the where and when of it may not be as obvious as you expect. Do not be discouraged if it does not all work at once – if you persevere it will.

The following exercise, called 'The Helmsman', puts you in control of your life and moves you closer to a sense of Purpose.

Relax and centre.

Imagine you are on a sailing ship, out in a vast ocean, with no land visible in any direction. Let yourself be carried by the ship, taking you where it will for a while.

Then let your sense of Purpose be present for you (even if, at this time, you are not that clear what your Purpose is). Just let yourself be filled with the sense of Purpose.

Then realise that you can be the helmsman on this ship, you can take control of the rudder and steer the ship in whatever direction seems most appropriate to you, so that you are travelling in a direction that leads you closer to your Purpose.

Take the helm, and be the helmsman. Vividly imagine yourself in this role, and allow yourself to fully enjoy the experience of being in control of your ship.

Blessing the Obstacle

At various times in our lives we all have the experience of failure. However hard we have tried to do something, it does not come off. The poet Bob Cobbing summed it up well once; he said life is like a tightrope act – sometimes it comes off, sometimes you come off!

When you experience failure it can lead to your cutting off your potential energy. You may be angry, bitter or disappointed. It is fine to feel these things, but it is also important, when you are ready, to move on, to allow the creative potential to flow once more. One important way for achieving this is through a process called 'blessing the obstacle'. You have to accept the failure, make a conscious act of blessing whatever has stopped you succeeding, and then move on. When you consider what you have learned from the apparent 'failure', the opportunity it has given you to do it again, whatever it is, only better this time, then it is not such a strange concept. If it is some act that now can never happen, then through blessing the obstacle you can come to the realisation that it obviously was not meant to happen. This is not an act of subordination to some impersonal fate, rather it is an act of conscious control and decision-making. You decide: if it does not happen, then you decided upon that, too, even if in your everyday consciousness, your personality, you have not been conscious of this process.

Instead of being a victim to pain or failure you can ask: What use is this to me? What can I learn from it?

Relax and centre.

Choose some recent pain or failure from your life, consider it in depth, bless the apparent obstacle (for example, simply by saying 'I bless this (fear or whatever)'), be aware of what you have learned from the situation, and consciously choose to move on.

You cannot always change the outer conditions but you can always work on the inner conditions. One way of doing this is through an act of acceptance. When we accept what is, we are open to learn. Indeed, acceptance is one of the most major tools for transformation. Think of a recent good experience. Spend some time recalling all the features of this experience – what you saw, heard, tasted, what you thought and felt at the time, exactly what was going on. Allow yourself to experience the pleasure associated with this good experience, whatever it was.

Now consider a recent 'bad' experience, something you did not feel good about. Again spend a little time recalling all the sensing, feeling and thinking associated with this time.

Now realise the value of both experiences.

The important thing is often not what is happening but our reaction to it – so turn and face it, whatever it is. See both successes and failures for what they are – events in the unfoldment of who you are. Gain a sense of perspective and proportion when you consider either, and always ask yourself: What choices can I make? How can I improve this in terms of my unfolding creative potential?

· 11 ·

OVERCOMING RESISTANCE
Exploring Glamour

It is obvious that an eagle's potential will be actualised in roaming the sky, diving down on smaller animals for food, and in building nests.
It is obvious that an elephant's potential will be actualised in size, power and clumsiness.
No eagle will want to be an elephant; no elephant to be an eagle. . . how absurd it would be if they, like humans, had fantasies, dissatisfactions, and self-deceptions. . .
Leave this to the human – to try to be something he is not, to have ideals that cannot be reached, to be cursed with perfectionism so as to be safe from criticism, and to open the road to unending mental torture.

FRITZ PERLS

There are various ways in which we deceive ourselves – either into believing we are 'worse' than we are or that we are 'better'than we are. Each person's experience and definition of themselves is different; we are all unique. The soul as it exists through us is both transcendent and immanent. In its immanent mode it deals with what is, dealing with things how they are; in its transcendent phase it pushes us beyond our limits, wants us to grow, to realise our potential for growth, beyond the limits of our current comprehension and experience. Both phases of the soul are proper to have; we need to co-operate and have a balance with both.

The personality walls itself with conscious and unconscious fears and blocks. It resists the playing out of the soul's Purpose, and this resistance creates glamour – to be something you are not, either worse or better than you are – and fear of your own growth and unfoldment. We will deal first with glamour as at some time or another we all fall victim to its enticement.

As long as you imagine you are the most important being in your world then you are cut off and cannot truly appreciate the world around you. This way you keep yourself apart from everyone and everything else. While essentially we are individual beings with our own soul, and our own personality, we are all, at the same time, connected to other human beings. Indeed, we are intimately connected to all living and non-living things throughout our universe. One obvious manifestation of this connectedness is through the groups to which we belong. We all belong to groups of various kinds, ranging from our family, in itself our primary group, being the first one most of us experience in life, through social and political groups, however diverse or vague our connections with these might feel, to our membership of the larger more abstract 'groups' such as humanity, primates, animals, living beings, inhabitants of the planet earth and so on.

We have at all times a sense of our involvement within each group, and further have a sense of responsibility to each group to which we belong. This responsibility affects our actions as individuals but also our actions as members of a community, a nation, a planet's inhabitants. None of our activities, however unique they may be to us, are in isolation from one or more of the groups to which we belong. At some level, to a greater or lesser degree, there will be some kind of interplay.

Glamour has been defined as the attribution of false values and exaggerated importance to people and situations – most frequently ourselves and our actions. Glamour can manifest in many varied guises; for example, possessiveness and self-interest. All glamours distort our perceptions, both about ourselves and about others. It is as if a glamour creates a veil which stops us viewing clearly what is really happening. As our perceptions are thus distorted we are unable to make clear and balanced decisions and actions, so, like a vicious circle, glamour breeds more glamour.

The concept of glamour includes all the deceptions, misunderstandings, misinterpretation and falsehood in which we believe. To be a victim of glamour is to be on one's own, living in a world inhabited by illusions and lies. Yet we may never see this. We may even share a particular world of glamour with others. For example, it is a glamour to believe that white-skinned people are superior in some way to other races. However ludicrous this may seem, many people will subscribe to this glamour, and their belief will be supported by other people who also hold this misconception. Such an illusion can become so strong it can become part of the belief structure of a whole group (for example, members of fascist parties), or a whole nation (for example, England during its imperialistic past). The fact that many individuals within the nation realise the falsity of this position in no way lessens the hold it may have on the national type. Dissenters from such nationally held beliefs may even be treated as outcasts or worse.

It is even possible, so it appears, for the whole planet to fall prey to a particularly strong glamour. It is not far from the truth to say that the vast majority of people on this planet believe human beings to be somehow superior to other animals. It certainly looks like this when we see how other species are treated. At all levels, whether local, national or global, various glamours pervade our lives and, to a frightening extent, influence our decisions and actions.

Each of us, as individuals and as members of various groups, are responsible for our blind adherence to glamours. We are also responsible for our own growth and our own liberation from these illusionary beliefs which hold us back from the total freedom to express ourselves. Glamours can often be most clearly seen through our emotionally based beliefs and attachments. They are reactive in nature rather than creative as true feelings are. For example, a true feeling of altruistic love may become distorted into a glamour of self-importance and ambition.

Some of the most common glamours which we can perceive acting upon us are:

> false authority
> personal ambition
> bigotry, certainty of being right
> false independence
> self-interest (at the expense of others)
> blinkered vision
> fanaticism
> possessiveness
> grandeur and self-importance
> pride

impatience
sense of inadequacy
fear
materialism
deviousness
vagueness
changeability
over-devotion
reluctance to change
rigidity
over-attachment

and so on – the list could be extended to infinity.

There are many techniques for lessening and even overcoming attachment to glamour, the chief ones being:

- dis-identification (you have learnt how to do this in a previous chapter; it is the prime method for dealing with glamours of all kinds);

- the recognition of reality;

- acting as if;

- the holding of right proportions;

- the cultivation of opposites;

We will now look at these various techniques, and see how we can apply them to our lives so that we can at least dissipate glamour if not eradicate it altogether.

The Recognition of Reality

Choose a glamour to which you feel strongly attached, perhaps from the list above.

Relax and centre.

Sit upright and meditate upon your chosen glamour. Keep your attention on its presence within you, and allow thoughts and images to arise that show you how this glamour affects your life. Do not become emotionally attached to what you see, simply observe the actions of this glamour upon your life.

Remaining calm, reflect on what you might do to free yourself from this glamour. If you wish, write down any connections you make or ideas you have for the dissipation of this particular glamour.

Visualise a bright light over your head which shines down through all the parts of your being, illuminating everything from the outermost reaches of your body to the innermost recesses of your soul. Identify with this light and let it fill your whole being. Recognise the reality of this light compared with the illusion of the glamour.

As it both completely envelops you and penetrates within you, allow the light to disperse the glamour. Vividly imagine the glamour leaving you and dissipating into space.

Say clearly and out loud; 'I remove myself from the influence of (name the glamour). As you say this stand up, stretch your body and deliberately and consciously choose to sit in another position.

See if you can think of acts you can perform which affirm your new connection to reality. Write in your diary about the experience.

Joan worked on her 'self-importance', a very common glamour. Don Juan says, in one of Carlos Castaneda's books: 'Self importance is our greatest enemy. . . what weakens us is feeling offended by the deeds or misdeeds of our fellow men. Our self importance requires that we spend most of our lives offended by someone.'

Joan realised her self-importance meant that, amongst other things, at work people did not really share either their ideas or their problems with her. In her position of authority she was isolated and generally only got to hear what people wanted her to hear. After working on this and connecting with the light, she realised there were many ways in which she could change this situation. For example, she could arrange weekly meetings in which all her employees could air their opinions and suggestions. She could come out of her office more and share some personal feelings about herself. Of course, the situation would not transform overnight, but through a definite, concerted effort she felt she could make improvements.

In fact, Joan did not find the change easy at all. There were some improvements but the old pattern was too deeply embedded for there to be real change at the rate she now desired. After a few months she undertook a total transformation. She now works for a different company where she is part of a team. The shared endeavour has brought a whole new quality of happiness to her life.

Acting As If

Relax and centre.

Choose a glamour to which you feel attached or which you feel you would particularly like to overcome.

Say to yourself: 'I realise I have (name the glamour). I am aware it is in me, that it limits me and harms me and those with whom I come into contact. As I am aware I have this glamour, I too am aware I do not have to have it. I can let it go. It is not part of my essential self. I do not not need it'.

Imagine a wave of light envelops you and, as it passes, it takes the glamour with it.

Imagine a situation in which you have exhibited 'your glamour'. For example, if it is 'possessiveness' visualise a situation where you have been possessive.

Let yourself feel the negativity your glamour has created, both in yourself and anyone else involved. As you visualise this scene or happening, imagine what it would have been like, how it would have been different if you had acted without attachment to the glamour.

Realise you could have acted as if the glamour was absent. The choice is always yours when you are conscious of your actions. Realise yourself as the director of your life play. You can act as if this glamour was absent from your acts and it will be so.

Of course, with a glamour that has strong attachments, you cannot expect it to dissipate in one easy go. You may have to repeat your affirmations and visualisations many times over before it is completely eradicated. But right from now you can act as if it is gone, and in so acting you can speed its removal.

You may feel there is the possibility that such an exercise may simply suppress or repress the glamour and you will not have dealt with it properly. If you simply ignored the problem this could be the case. Using this technique, however, you remain very conscious of its presence and you act as if is not present in order to transform the energy, not to ignore it.

Michael chose 'impatience' as a particularly insidious glamour to which he felt attached. He visualised a scene in which he was being impatient with his wife whom he felt at that time was being too slow getting ready to go out for the evening. Although he knew it was really quite a trivial matter he allowed his impatience to take him over. They ended up arguing, this delayed their departure even more, and the resultant bad feelings marred their enjoyment of an evening with friends. They did not really make it up until they got home, went to bed and made love.

When he re-visualised the scene without impatience, he saw himself relaxed, taking the time to do some little chore he wanted to complete instead of idly waiting. They were still a little late leaving home, but their relations were more harmonious, they arrived at their friends on time and had an engaging and interesting evening. When they arrived home they went to bad happy and relaxed. They made love from a place of compassion and continued togetherness rather than from a place of separation, as a way of making it up. Mike realised he much preferred this way. His impatience would not disappear overnight, but he was on the road towards its transformation.

The Holding of Right Proportions

At times we all let events in our inner or outer lives become blown up out of all proportion. This can happen in various ways. Perhaps you are angry at someone over something they have done, and, almost as if it is a game, you allow yourself to let rip in a way that is out of proportion with the incident. On the other hand, such disproportionate behaviour is often much less conscious. When it happens you feel that you are justifiably angry, or whatever, and certainly do not feel as if you are 'overdoing it'. It can happen over the simplest little things. Your lover brings you an apple when you wanted an orange and all hell lets rip. She does not really love you at all, she never attends to your needs properly, she does not listen, she is so selfish . . .!

At such times you have the opportunity to look at this behaviour. Ask yourself, when you catch yourself in such a situation: Who is this other person? Who am I 'really' angry at? Perhaps you are projecting a parent on to this other person, and really you are shouting at your mother, say, who did not pick you up every time you wanted when you were a baby. The point of this is not to analyse what the reasons are beyond your behaviour, but to connect you to a sense of right proportions. Once you see, hear and feel in proportion to the situation you no longer 'need' to over-react.

As a corollary to this, when you get such a sense of right proportions, you will find you can also react strongly when it is appropriate, and let rip when it is right to do so!

If you live with another person, or if there is someone with whom you spend a fair amount of time, it can be useful for you both to make an agreement that whenever you notice your pattern, or he or she notices you in such a situation, remember to ask that person: How old do you feel right now? For this to be effective it must be a true two-way agreement, you must not use such a technique just to 'get at' the other person. You are not saying: You are acting childishly. You are giving the other person the opportunity to stop, look at themselves and see what is happening inside. When you are asked the question about how old you feel, you should answer instantly. Do not think about it, just see what age comes to you. You might be surprised.

The Cultivation of Opposites

You do not have to be a bigot to believe you are right about something, yet all beliefs are truly relative. Of course, most of us will subscribe to a belief that old people should not be beaten up and robbed of their pensions. But what of more subtle or less distinct beliefs, or beliefs that are in some way idiosyncratic? You have a right to believe whatever you choose to believe so long as you do not ever try to impose that belief on someone else without their permission. I might believe it is good to meditate every morning, but if I impose that on you, apart from the fact it is only a belief, my trying to impose it will probably make you react against it anyway.

We need to cultivate opposites to overcome this (and be careful, this is just a belief in itself!). It has been suggested as good practice to 'marry each thought against its opposite'. If you attempt this, you have to take care not to be left in a position of 'neither this, nor that' or where your response is habitually 'yes. . . but. . .' to everything, a place from where it is impossible to make clear decisions. But it is useful as a technique to apply when appropriate. Should you meditate every morning at six o'clock? Yes and no. You believe that all people are created equal. On the other hand, you know that we are all individuals and our individuality makes us essentially different from everyone else. If wealth ('well-th') is something which enhances life in some way, then 'illth' is the opposite, something which distracts from and lessens life. Through keeping you separate, afraid and disconnected from the true unlimited source within you, all glamours have this effect.

For example, we might fall prey to the glamour of regression: this accepts soul but distorts it. You might feel, for example, that you do not have to work anymore, you are in touch, you trust in God and that is all you need. You want it all to be easy, you want the benefits without the work. It is as if you are returning to an undifferentiated state rather than accepting differentiation and bringing soul into that. There is a big difference between being childlike and childish.

Another similarly insidious glamour is rationalisation: explaining it all away with 'yes but', 'only if' and so forth. Or you can negate what is inside you, denying the existence of soul, and inner energy, even violently. Sometimes this becomes clear when you 'protest too much' and other people clearly see how you really have what you are so vehemently denying.

Or you might fall prey to 'retrospective devaluation' – well, it seemed important at the time, but now I realise I was fooling myself. It was to do with the time of day, the state I was in, the food I had eaten, my emotional instability – due to anything other than the playing out of the soul's Purpose. A lack of trust in your own soul can lead you to desacralisation – always looking for the flaws or faults in people, events, or systems. Sarcasm is a form of this kind of defence. Scepticism is a very healthy trait; sarcasm is crass defensiveness.

The opposite of this is dogmatisation and bigotry. You 'know' that this is the only way; all other ways are false, illusionary, not true to the tradition, mistaken, even intentionally false and evil. We might drill our own wells but we need to realise that we all tap into the same water underneath. Yet people build a church over their well and think this is the only truly holy water. They then end up honouring the well rather than the water.

Of course, it is possible that our connections are illusionary, our realisations are falsehoods, or, alternatively, that our way is the one and only true way. But in either case it would still be true to say that other people have to find their own way, and if we or they have fallen prey to illusion and glamour then that is what is, and today, tomorrow, next century or next lifetime we or they will awaken. The ultimate glamour is not to think you are right or wrong, but to try to impose your beliefs on someone else.

Walls of Fear

Many of our walls against effective functioning are built from our fears of being who we really are. To overcome this resistance fully you need to face these fears and transform them, allowing their energy to be released and be an asset rather than a hindrance to your free expression and experience of yourself as a soul incarnating through a personality. The main walls of fear we see operating in ourselves are described next. Look at these fears and assess for yourself how you exhibit them, if at all, then see if you can devise techniques or actions that will help you overcome them. This will take a great act of courage, but if you truly wish to overcome fear you have to make such acts. You cannot just wish fears away. For instance, if you fear losing your individuality, find a situation where you can temporarily (and safely) let go of your individuality and see what it feels like. You might, for example, join a drama group where you have to 'play someone else' to someone else's direction. Or you might find a team sport which involves letting go of your individual needs so that you can help the whole team.

The more physical ways you can find of facing these fears, the more they dissipate. If you have faced your fear of losing individuality, for example, when moments arise in your consciousness where it is appropriate for you to let go – to merge with a cosmic wave of universality perhaps – you will be able to take such action more easily. You can only learn to surrender through surrendering! So find the ways in which you can do something you fear, and the ways in which you cannot do it will become easier to face.

FEAR OF RESPONSIBILITY

If we are going to be truly ourselves it entails a certain responsibility, a heavy-duty responsibility. This can be too much and we shy away from it, or we build a false wall around such beliefs as: I cannot be that until I've worked through such and such, this amount of 'shit' needs to be overcome before I can possibly be myself.

Ask yourself: Can I handle the responsibility of not being true to my soul?

FEAR OF BEING OVERWHELMED

I cannot handle the bigger responsibility it entails to be the soul. I will be overwhelmed, I'll even die.

Ask yourself: Is it really so bad to be overwhelmed? How do I know this?

FEAR OF BEING BURDENED

If I am aware of it I have to do something about it, so I shall avoid it at all costs, even if it means my life ends up being meaningless and boring – that is better than being burdened! Maslow said 'the avoidance of knowledge is the avoidance of responsibility'.

Ask yourself: Is it better to have tried and even failed than not to have attempted anything?

FEAR OF LOSING INDIVIDUALITY

It is possible to fear surrendering to the universal, to want it to be 'my will' rather than 'thy will' that is done. It is important here to distinguish between true individuality (that you connect to as a soul), and the individuality of personality (that is transient and illusionary). If it were possible to lose your soul that would be a calamity, but to lose your separateness and false boundaries can be a blessing. The whole issue of boundaries is very complex, and dealt with elsewhere in this book. It may seem paradoxical in a book like this which is constantly stressing the importance of individuality and being oneself to say you have to lose your individuality, but when you truly connect this paradox appears quite sane.

Ask yourself: When I really tune in to my centre, my self, is there any distinction between my will and Spiritual Will?

FEAR OF IMPOTENCY

The fear of being powerless, of being a victim to the universe, or to circumstances beyond our control, is rife in our modern world. Our political leaders encourage it and thrive upon it. It causes us to hold on strongly to what we have got and not let the new in. It is as if we defend ourselves against what we really are. When you connect how can you be impotent?

Ask yourself: Is there anything I can do that is not an unfoldment of the universal pattern?

FEAR OF DEATH

This can be connected to other fears or directly relevant in itself. It is the individuality that fears dying, yet in one sense we truly die each day many times over, as we change and grow and become different. Even in a physical sense we have many millions of cells dying within us each day. In around seven years from now every single cell in your entire body will have been replaced by a new one. Yet there is that which remains. You can choose to embrace death gladly and excitedly each day.

Ask yourself: What can I find in myself that is everlasting?

FEAR OF POWER (HAVING IT OR MISUSING IT)

If we resist our inner strength, our power, we are not making a real distinction between personal and soul power. Personal power comes and goes, but soul power remains (whether we lose our awareness of it or not). If it is always there is it not better to utilise it than fear it?

But you might misuse your power if you connect to it and use it. You might end up hurting others. 'I don't want to be who I am because I might hurt someone,' is a commonly held distortion. You may fear intruding on another person's process in an inappropriate way, even harmfully. You need to recognise you are a soul, you are the source in your universe.

The process of life can be trusted, through inclusion, centring and synthesis.

Ask yourself: How many people do I hurt through not being myself?

FEAR OF LIFE DISRUPTION

'It's cosy now, if I let this in I might be lonely, I might lose my friends and my nice comfortable life. . .' This is true, you might, but is your ordinary everyday life really so safe, so warm, so comfortable that you do not want to strive for something more? Usually the changes are more gradual than this anyway, and you have time to adjust to new ways of being and doing.

Ask yourself: Am I doing this alone, or are there others just like me?

FEAR OF INADEQUACY

Even Jesus asked for his 'cup' to be taken from him, and what an example to us this story is. You may not, in your personality, feel adequate, or deserving, or 'good enough', but your Purpose, once you have connected to it, will not be removed or baulked at. Stop looking for results, just follow your course a step at a time, and you will find all the energy you need. Use exercises and techniques like the ones presented in this book to connect to your Purpose and move towards your soul, then see what brings you joy.

You can imagine that you have to be perfect before you can serve, indeed, before you can be truly yourself. Yet perfection is just being who you are; all the so-called 'good' aspects and 'bad' aspects are all perfect for you at this moment. Allow and trust a lot more in yourself as you are.

Ask yourself: How can I be inadequate when I am what I am?

FEAR OF BEING WRONG

It might all be illusion, a glamour. What if you are fooling yourself?

No way is the right or the wrong way. A zen monk lived in a town which was called in Japanese 'The Right Place to Live'. A visiting dignitary looked at the poverty, squalor and starvation in the town and asked the monk – how on earth can this be the right place to live? The monk responded by saying that when you realise this place is neither the right place nor the wrong place to live, you can truly realise it is 'The Right Place to Live'.

Ask yourself: Can I be anywhere else but home?

FEAR OF SUCCESS

The most insidious fear of all is the fear of success, of being who you really are. You can work on this by developing your will, through dis-identification, and actively working on the expression of your Purpose in a calmer, more centred way. This allows you to manifest and use your energy from your soul more effectively, instead of being diverted and distracted.

Ask yourself: Truly, in my heart, would I like to succeed or fail?

FEAR OF THE UNKNOWN

It is impossible to be afraid of the unknown. If you do not know it you have no way of being afraid of it, except through fantasy. And you can control fantasy so anything becomes either threatening or enhancing, positive or negative. You have this control. Do not reject something because it's not you as you are now. Whatever it is, you can become it. Potential is truly unlimited.

Ask yourself: Is fear itself the only thing to fear?

· 12 ·

TOUCH DOWN
Exploring The Ground

Ordinary life is not safe. . . ordinary life does not provide us with enough meaning after a certain point: we must look for self-actuality, for spiritual growth, or experience the living death of emptiness.

CHARLES TART

Purpose comes from the self, through the soul, and tries to manifest through the personality into the world. So long as it is not grounded it is ineffective. Without a connection to ground it does not happen. We need to connect with our purpose and effectively translate that purpose into clear intention – that is, to know, feel and sense what we are going to do. Intention is different from motivation. Intention comes from a connection to purpose, from inside of ourselves. Motivations, on the other hand, come from our responses to the outside world, and are 'chosen' by subpersonalities. Motivation and intention can, of course, be the same thing, or can be connected, but usually they are not.

Remember an earlier chapter where you learned the difference between wanting something and needing it? Wants are usually exclusive and are what motivate us. They are a response, often a victim kind of response. Intentions, on the other hand, are more about fulfilling role and purpose. I want a chocolate bar and nothing else will do. It motivates me to act. Or I need something to eat and it is my intention to fulfil that need in the best way I know how, not through eating chocolate but through choosing a more healthy alternative.

Whether we are talking about purpose, intention or motivation, we need a definite plan to fulfil it, to get it. We need to make a link between the intention and what is intended. This is called the magical link, and is in essence our ability to 'bring into manifestation' whatever it is we wish to ground. We enter here into the realms of magick – not as something weird or 'occult' but as the way of connecting with 'higher' energies and using them as we wish.

The Magical Link

We will now explore the 'Magical Link', a way of grounding or manifesting energy. To bring anything into manifestation there are always four stages to the process.

1. *Banishing* relates to the intellect, and means that all other ideas apart from the matter at hand must be banished. This is mainly achieved through singlemindedness.
2. *Purifying* relates to the feelings, and refers to purification of the emotions.
3. *Consecrating* relates to the individual self, and involves being dedicated to a single purpose.
4. *Grounding* or 'bringing into manifestation', relates to the earth or 'ground'. There is no point in banishing thoughts, purifying feelings and consecrating the purpose and oneself, if you do not ground the energy, and bring about the desired change.

Any desired change can be most effectively realised through a 'magical link', where magick is defined as any act brought to pass by will. For the magick to work, the link must be properly made, that is, the appropriate means used in the appropriate measure, and applied in ways pertinent to the purpose, through an 'agency' that connects the willer to the desired object. For example, a young man may have an unswerving desire to have a girlfriend, and there might be a girl with a strong desire to be his girlfriend, but unless the link is made the will of both will be unfulfilled forever. Or imagine I want some fruit from a local shop. I know the means for getting there (walking), the right direction (turn left, right, then right again), the correct pressure to apply in the right direction (that is, forward at 4 mph in a determined manner) – all the details are there for me to fulfil my will and purchase the fruit *except the magical link*. Unless, when I get to the shop, I can make a magical link with the shopkeeper I will not get the fruit. In this case the magic link will be a talisman (of a particular kind, usually called 'money'!).

There are two kinds of magical link – those that take place 'inside you' and those that involve 'outside you'. Inner links are those made within your own body. They are the easiest in the sense that everything needed is contained within the system, and perhaps the hardest in that internal inertia has to be overcome. Without the will you would not be able to do anything. If your will disappeared right now you would be forever chained to the place and position you are now in!

However, despite this condition, for any 'purpose' you choose with inner work, whether it is spiritual or material in orientation, you have all the necessary energies within. With outer links this is not so – there has to be a connector between you and the object of your will, such as the money to buy the fruit in the example given.

Sometimes inner force itself can make the link, for example if you express your true love for someone a link might be made, assuming that person feels the strength of your love and it connects with their love for you. All the qualities of the soul (truth, joy, beauty, etc.) *if they are made manifest in the personality* become links in themselves.

In one way or another, with both internal and external work, the link has to be made. This cannot be stressed too often. The most frequently used method of creating a link is through grounding, which gives the energy you wish to manifest a 'place' in which to manifest itself.

There are several easy ways to ground energy:

- simply by expressing the experience;
- writing, and/or drawing;
- evening reviews or morning previews (going over the past or coming day and looking how you performed, not as a judgmental exercise but in order that you might function more effectively through knowledge of how you habitually perform);
- construction of 'talismans' (or using existing ones as in the money example above);
- acting as if – in other words acting as if the desired end has already happened (see Chapter 11);

- meditation, either on the object of the will itself or a symbol you have constructed to represent the will;
- evocative word-cards; sometimes called 'self-advertising' – you write your desire (in words or symbols) on postcards and stick them up around your home in places where you will frequently see them – just as with commercial advertising, constant exposure has an effect on the unconscious;
- free drawing or automatic drawing;
- creating a suitable (psychological) environment;
- creating a mantra and constantly chanting or repeating it to yourself;
- specific creations in life, for example going to beautiful places;
- finding an object to represent what happened.

The aim of grounding is the 'anchoring of evolution'. The soul is evolving, it is our wish to help in that process by taking responsibility for the creation of our life, using our will to fulfil our real inner needs, and to ground our inspirations and insights. We need to create the form that allows the energy to come through. If it is a circular energy then we need a circular form for it, a triangular one will not do. This is the work of the personality, to make the right shape for energy to manifest. The most effective ways of grounding energy come from your own life situations. If you have never gone fishing there is little point (in the short term anyway) of grounding a need for fish through fishing. You would do better to fit the need into your life situation and experience, that is, go to the local supermarket!

Insights come through the mind, the feelings or the body. In the mind they take the form of 'ahas', flashes, understanding in a conceptual way; through the feelings they are experienced as qualities, energies, colours, and so on; through the body as sensations. The techniques for grounding are many, and best directly discovered through your own living connections. But there are some commonly known ways at least to assist the grounding and perhaps achieve it fully, as described above. In essence what you need to do is formulate the experience clearly in your consciousness. Ask yourself: What does this mean, how does it fit into my life, my experience, what would my life be like if that insight or desire was actualised?

You are now going to learn a way of 'hooking yourself to the centre of the earth'.

Relax and centre.

Sit upright, let the base of your spine become really heavy, and see it as an anchor. Imagine the anchor goes down into the earth, attached by a light but strong cord to your whole body. Let it pass in its own way through layers of rock and sediment and anything else it comes to until it finally reaches the core of the earth, then hook it in there. Let it find its own way down and hook to centre in a natural way; do not force it.

Feel yourself hooked into the planet's core, the planet's energy of which you are a part.

You can extend this exercise by having your feet flat on the ground, and imagining that they have openings on the bottom. Draw energy up through them as you inhale; circulate this energy through your body, then as you exhale let it go back down into the earth. Then you are circulating earth energy through your body. Cycling and recycling this energy will really connect you to the earth.

We are all, individually, a bit like 'growths' on the earth's surface, little 'blips' sticking out, like hairs on the globe-shaped body of our mother planet. Each 'hair' or 'blip' is as important as any other and each hair has the potential to grow to its fullest height. You can let this happen through you.

Connection

In life we are 'processors' or 'dynamos' of energy, each of us interacting with a total 'sea' of energy that fills us up, surrounds us, and composes everything (and every 'non-thing'!) in our world. Through this sea of energy, we are all connected. Our separation is an illusion, but most definitely a necessary and useful illusion that helps us be ourselves and manifest our purpose. The problem comes when either we can no longer connect with this sea, or if we can not separate ourselves from it. Too little or too much connection are equally undesirable states.

Relax and centre.

Choose a soul quality that you feel you connect with quite clearly, and that you would wish to share with everyone and everything else. It might be joy, truth, beauty, peace – anything. Then quite simply choose to radiate it out from yourself. You might like to hold your arms out, with your palms in a gesture of giving, you might like to use some words, or you might simply prefer to do it silently, in imagination. There is no right or wrong way to do this; indeed, it will be most effective if you find your own way.

After a group therapy session which involved the expression of deep inner emotions, Keith felt very lonely. He walked home across a park, tears filling his eyes. He says he felt as if no one in the whole universe could possibly understand his state. It was as if he were an alien, stranded on a distant planet where no one even saw him or heard him, let alone was able to communicate with him. When he got home to his flat, he laid on his bed and allowed these feelings and emotions to engulf him. He sobbed and sobbed.

Gradually Keith felt a new sense of loneliness coming over him, now transformed, in a sense, into 'alone-ness'. Connecting with this new feeling, he realised it was not part of his purpose to be connected all the time. Part of his lesson for this life was to learn to be alone without being lonely. His spirits were raised and, feeling a rush of energy, he realised he was being healed. He allowed the energy to build then, suddenly, and quite spontaneously, he stood up, raised his left hand and, holding it out before him, saw it bathed in a clear, blue light.

He intuitively knew what to do. Raising his hand high, with his palm facing out, he visualised a stream of yellow light flowing through him and going out into the world, a light of healing and blessing to the planet. Keith felt fulfilled – still alone, in the deepest sense, but, at the same time, connected through his energy to everyone and everything else. By allowing his alone-ness he had connected in a truly meaningful way.

If you want to radiate out positive energy in this way, you may find that other colours than those used by Keith are more effective for you. Also it is important to protect yourself from negative energies that can flow back into you. The most effective way of doing this is to imagine you are enclosed with a bright but dark blue egg of protective light, perhaps with little silver stars twinkling on the periphery. The more often you visualise yourself surrounded by such an egg the more protected you become from unwanted psychic intrusions.

Intuition

Intuition is very different from 'psychic intrusion', and comes when a contact is made between soul and your personality, your 'divinity' and your 'humanity'. To be able to receive intuitions fully and clearly, however, you need to work on your personality so that they are received in a harmonious way, with as little distortion as possible. Your receptacle has to be suitable or the messages you receive will be unclear.

When we investigate the functions of our brains, and look at the different modes of thought of which we are capable, we initially see a primary split between abstract and concrete functions. There are no sharp divisions between these two, rather a more gradual division where one merges into the other, but they can, for convenience, be viewed separately.

We hear a lot these days about the right and left brain functions (although some recent research suggests this is far too simplistic a model of brain functioning). Whether it is a good description or not in terms of the actual physical organ we call a brain, it is a useful division to help us understand the abstract and concrete thinking modes that we all call experience.

The left brain (connecting to the right side of the body) is concerned with rational and linear modes of operation. From the left brain you think, order, make lists and organise your life and actions. It is from here that concrete thinking takes place. The right brain (connecting to the left side of the body), is concerned with non-rational, intuitive, non-linear modes of operation. From the right brain you feel, intuit, make crazy connections, and generally live in a non-ordered, more fluid way. Both sides are of equal importance and both are equally necessary for the full and healthy functioning of the individual. Problems only arise when one assumes an unhealthy dominance over the other, or there is a critical identification with one or other of the ways of operating.

Concrete functions (left brain, thinking and sensing) involve physical matters, they help us to understand our actual, physical existence, our functioning here on the planet earth, in this dense earthy energy. Abstract functions (right brain, intuiting and feeling) involve making connections in a non-linear, non-verbal way, helping to increase our awareness and process our expression of who we really are.

We are all moving towards greater awareness. Anything abstract, or non-manifest, can come to life through a number of forms. It can emerge through your thoughts, feelings or body, perhaps as a 'sense' or 'feeling' or 'flash' of knowledge and understanding. Patterns are trying to emerge, and the more we are open to their emergence, without trying to force them into a particular form, the better they are able to emerge. If a triangle is emerging you will receive its wisdom more easily, and more clearly, if you can create a triangular receptor in your being with which to receive it. Fitting squares into round holes is a far more difficult, and daunting proposition. In other words, the more we do to connect with our deeper, innermost nature, and the more we create a well-functioning personality, the better able we are to receive or channel the inner wisdom and unfoldment of purpose which is inevitably trying to emerge into consciousness.

Relax and centre.

Think back over this day and ask yourself: What am I doing here? What is the meaning in all the things I have done today? Try to perceive an underlying pattern behind all areas of action and focus through your day. Spend some time on this, reflecting on these emerging patterns and actions in life.

Now abstract from this particular day and see the events you have been considering within a wider context. See your life as a whole.

Everything you think is a belief, a mental construct. What time of day is it? What day of the week? Answers to all such questions involve a belief, a mental construct, about the meaning of time and space, being here as opposed to there, being now as opposed to then. Being on this beautiful planet in this vast universe is also a construct, everything is a construct. Being in a galaxy, on a planet, in a house, in this room, all these ideas are constructs. The kind of person you believe you are – this is a construct, different from the simple perception of being. The world you live in, this is a construct, too. Remember that constructs are not 'real' in any concrete sense and can be changed. Do you like the world you live in? Do you like the 'game' you are playing?

Yet some constructs can seem more right than others. Look for this rightness, and hold these constructs. Let others go, and constantly revise your position on what you 'know' to be true, what you believe in and what you do not. If you are not flexible you are rigid and rigid things break under stress. A Taoist sage once told a monk that a twisted tree they were passing was very wise. When asked to explain, he said that the trees that grow up perfectly straight and strong get cut down for use as firewood, for furniture, boats or whatever. This tree, by going with the flow of nature, bending this way with the winds and that way with the rains, had grown up twisted and gnarled, but had been left to its own devices, to grow as it chose, and had not been cut down or used. Its trust in the flow of nature had ensured it a long life.

You can find those moments when you connect with a sense of rightness. This is a form of intuition, of which there are basically three kinds:

1. 'I know but I don't know why' – a kind of common sense that comes through your thoughts, feelings or body. We often distrust these intuitions as being 'fantasy' or imagination, which, of course, sometimes they are. On the other hand, though, we can learn to separate those we can trust from those that are fantasies through using our discriminative faculties. If you still yourself and look at your thoughts and feelings about the situation, sometimes it becomes easier to tell if this 'knowing' is genuine intuition or something you have created in your imagination without a connection to a deeper level of knowledge.

2. 'I have a sense it is right' – this 'sense' comes into the superconscious, and is to do with rightness and choice. For it to manifest, you have to look at the most holistic, largest vision you hold. Without a connection to this 'larger picture' it is too easy to have all kinds of 'senses' about situations or people that are way off mark. If you hold your connection to your deeper or innermost self, then you can trust that your intuitions are in line with 'the highest good'.

3. 'It came to me in a flash'. These intuitions include major insights, glimpses of an intuitive plan at the highest level, and can manifest directly or through great music, works of art or even in the most unexpected and strange ways, for example, when synchronistic events occur or strange connections are made between you and someone or something else. The nature of this kind of intuitive insight leaves little doubt about the veracity of its message, for a true 'flash' enters your consciousness with enough light to make itself felt in an unambiguous way. If there is any ambiguity then you have to question where the intuition came from and whether it is truly guidance from the soul.

All your beliefs or 'world views' you probably learned as a child, from parents, the church, school teachers and so on. You might not consciously believe them anymore, but unless you work on them they are still there as unconscious constructs and will affect your life, and can at least potentially, and in most cases most definitely, hold you back from expressing who you truly are. And it is essential to remember there is no right answer to anything, just different points of view.

It is important to watch for assumptions in this process. For example, fear is an assumption something will go wrong, or at least possibly go wrong. Can it? Mistrust is an assumption that there is no order or plan in the universe. Isn't there? How do you know either way? Frustration is an assumption that there is an alternative way to do things. Yet if there is an alternative way of doing things, what is there to be frustrated about?

If a construct is a map then it is fine, it can help you find out where you are and connect you to where you wish to go. On the other hand if it affects and colours the territory then it is no longer enhancing to you or your life. It is as simple and as complicated as that.

Think deeply about everything you know, people, places, anything that comes to mind. Allow your thoughts to run as free associations, without censoring anything and, as far as possible, without judging anything. Let this process continue for some time, then ask: Who is aware of all these thoughts?

There is only one being, there is only one awareness. This unity is becoming increasingly manifest. The soul is increasingly manifesting through you. Come back into your life with this awareness and ground it.

· 13 ·

Subtle Bodies
Exploring Energy

The more pieces of our puzzle we gather, the more we begin to realise what a puzzle we really are. Even when all the pieces are placed, it's still a puzzle. . . a mystery to be lived and not a problem to be figured out.

ANTERO ALLI

There is no denying the energy in our physical bodies. For a start, there is all the energy we use, usually totally unconsciously, in order to stay alive, and hopefully thrive. We take in oxygen and various foods, then transform these substances into energy. We use this energy to sustain ourselves, replace cells, mend wounds, run the pump we call the heart, and so on. After these essential functions, we have energy to spare, that we could call potential energy. We can use it in a variety of ways – to sell vegetables to our customers, to saw wood for a fire, to 'pump iron' or practice karate, to 'push a pen', to make love. . .

Esoteric psychology says there is another body, closely associated with and aligned to the physical body, called the etheric body. This is your 'double' as it were, on a physical level, but composed of energy. If we could see the planet from outer space, we could see its 'physical body'. But if we had a different vision through which we could see not the physical earth but the energy generated by all the actions taking place all over the earth, we would be seeing the 'etheric body' of the planet. It is the same for individual people. We see our physical body as a whole, but if we could see all the energy being generated within us, as a separate entity, as it were, then we would be seeing the etheric 'double'. We not only have this double, but we are able to 'tune into' it, as a separate entity, and some people are able to separate it, move it around, and have direct experiences with this body.

We all affect our etheric bodies at all times, however. What you eat, what physical situations you are in, and what acts you are performing, all affect the energy produced in your body. Everything you do on a physical level affects you on a primary energy level. The etheric is looped with the physical in such a way that the etheric also affects the physical. What energy exchanges take place on the etheric directly affect the corresponding part of the physical body. So, for example, if a healer could affect the etheric, energy body it would effect a change on the physical.

We do not just have two bodies, however. Just as there is an energy body, the etheric, associated with the physical body, and the world of sensation, so, too, there are subtle bodies associated with the feeling and thinking functions of our personality, and, of course, the soul and spiritual bodies. The subtle body associated with the personality, and most particularly with the emotions, is the astral body. This too, while closely interwoven with the functioning of the personality through the thoughts, feelings and emotions (the most obviously energetically charged personality function), is yet a distinct body in its own right. Like the etheric, it can be independently disassociated from the physical individual, or apparently so. Astral travel is often confused (by 'esoteric' writers) with the separation of the etheric double from the body. Stories about a ghost-like double leaving the physical body, often attached by a silver thread or golden cord, are descriptions of the separation of the etheric double from the physical body. It can be a dangerous practice, though this is rare so long as care is taken (by those able to accomplish this difficult technique).

Astral travel, or 'vision', on the other hand, is rarely if ever dangerous (to the physical being, anyway), and involves not so much a separation of bodies, but an 'imaginative disassociation of consciousness'. You know you are still sitting in your chair and you could, if you wanted, open your eyes and be back immediately, but you are 'in another world' inside, seeing what is happening there and having experiences that, on that imaginative level, are very real. All of the exercises in this book asking you to visualise yourself in another world (in a meadow for example), have been exercises in astral vision.

To summarise, we have the following 'bodies':

The Subtle Body	'Physical' Counterpart
etheric	manifest body
astral	emotions and thoughts
soul	the heart
spirit	the crown

All our bodies, both physical and subtle ones, are not really separate, but form a continuum from the physical outwards. The relationship between the abstract and concrete mind is analogous to the relationship between the etheric and physical bodies. Just as the concrete mind is built upon the abstract, and not vice versa, so it is the same with the subtle bodies. The physical is built upon the etheric, is built upon the astral, is built upon the spiritual. They operate at different rates of vibration.

You can perform quite simple exercises which enable you to separate your physical body from your astral body. The key is in getting it to do different acts from the physical body.

For example, stand up straight, then step a few times, deliberately and consciously, to the left. Then continue doing this but, with your imagination, see and feel your astral body moving in the opposite direction to the right. Try this with different parts of your body, and allow your imagination free rein to really sense your astral as moving separately from your physical body.

The simplest way to separate your astral body is to lie down, relax, breathe deeply, imagine yourself in a meadow, then explore the inner territory you are creating. You have done this already in exercises throughout this book. The 'body' you use for this exploration is the astral.

Much is spoken of astral vision, but the astral has all the senses that the physical has, fully developed at least in potential, and maybe it has more. To experience this you might try, for instance, smelling something near you with your physical nose. Then imagine you can smell something at some distance. You might like to imagine the smell of toothpaste (which, unless you brush your teeth while reading this will not be in your immediate vicinity!). Then smell something at a greater distance – what does it smell like outside a nearby restaurant? Really experience the smell as if you are right there. Use your other senses, through imagination, to heighten the experience. If you visualise freshly baked apple pie you might just smell it! This will be accomplished through the astral, which allows to create, as it were, things 'out of thin air'.

You do not have to limit your imaginative faculties to what you have previously experienced. Try to smell the scents of outer space. No one might 'really' know what it smells like in outer space, but that in no way lessens the validity of your astral experience. No one knows what, say, freshly grown grass 'really' smells like either. All we can know is our personal perception of anything we experience. So you can choose to have the experiences that you want to have. The implications of this are quite staggering.

Finally, you might like to try this with the actual, physical world inside your body – what does your heart actually look like, smell like, taste like?

The Etheric

The etheric is so closely interwoven with the physical it is often difficult to distinguish the experience of each. Everything that happens to the physical body happens to the etheric, and vice versa, but at a different vibration. If you can affect the etheric in a positive way, it will affect the physical in a similar or corresponding way. Unfortunately the reverse is also true.

If you affect the etheric it will 'seep through' and affect the physical. If you become ill with, say, a cold or flu, on a physical level it is clearly caused by a bacterium or virus, which, although it might not be completely identifiable through the methods of science, will none the less be generally considered to 'actually exist'. This cannot really be doubted on the physical plane. On the etheric plane, however, it is possible to see other causes for illness and physical discomfort. At certain times in the past, people have thought that 'demons' cause illness. This is not so far from the truth, for the etheric double of viruses does appear, to certain sensitives, to be very demonic in appearance.

To speak of demons causing illness may only be a metaphor, but, if we believe that affecting something on the etheric will affect the physical in a corresponding way, perhaps the banishing or exorcism of an etheric demon may have the required effect. This way of looking at illness, particularly those 'incurable' by conventional means, may well be worth consideration.

If someone makes a sudden loud sound you might 'jump out of your skin' – this is an experience of the etheric body being temporarily detached from the physical. Similarly, you might feel you 'leave your stomach behind' as you hurtle down a roller coaster at the fair – this 'stomach' you leave behind is your etheric double!

Healing Energies

You can combine the imaginative skill of the astral with the causative faculties of the etheric to create healing energies.

One simple way of practising this is to move a finger of one hand closer and closer to the finger of your other hand, until they are nearly but not quite touching, and 'feel' the etheric double of each. Be aware of when the etheric boundary is reached, then when the etheric of each finger becomes intermingled.

You can also extend your etheric by simply imagining this. Reach out with your physical hand towards something just out of your reach, then imagine your etheric extends further than your physical can and touches the object. With practice you can begin to 'pick up' sensations from such 'etheric touch'.

When you feel confident with extending your etheric double in this way, you can start healing, but at first keep it simple and only on yourself. For example, if you have a bruise or cut, use your etheric to facilitate the required healing. By extending your etheric until it is covering the 'wound', then imagining it is filled with healing energy and light, you can assist the body's own healing functions. Do not attempt to heal other people in this way until you are very experienced and feel totally at tune with your etheric. The problem could be that, unless you are really strong and clear in only sending out positive healing energy it is possible to end up receiving the negative energy from the other person and become ill yourself. This, unfortunately, does happen to many ungrounded psychics and healers (often indicated physically by a fattening and lack of tone in the body).

Another useful technique for using the etheric for healing involves both the etheric and the physical bodies together. You simply 'push' into the flesh on your own or the client's body until it feels like even pressure or resistance both ways – there is a balance where the resistance of the flesh pushing back to you equals the pressure you are extending inwards. Contact is made like this. Then you can extend your etheric to send energy into the person.

Clairvoyance happens when physical and etheric consciousness overlap, as it were, and 'seeing' is accentuated into this 'sixth sense'.

The Chakras

Inside our bodies are innumerable 'power points' of which there are seven major ones called chakras (or 'wheels of energy'). All wheels are chakras – galaxies are chakras and the whole universe is a chakra. The chakras within our bodies are the energy centres or 'power stations' of the human body. A chakra may be either closed or open, and when it is open it gives the individual powers of perception and creativity. The seven major body chakras are:

Energy Centre	Name
base of spine	muladhara
genital	svadisthana
belly	manipura
heart	anahata
throat	visuddhi
midhead	ajna

Energy Centre   **Name**
top of head   sahasara

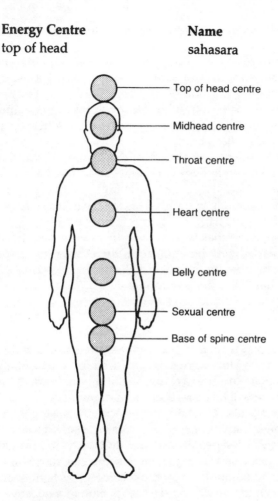

Top of head centre

Midhead centre

Throat centre

Heart centre

Belly centre

Sexual centre

Base of spine centre

Figure 7: The Body and Chakras

There are more chakras than the seven 'major' ones, and these are sometimes called 'minor' chakras (a comment on their position within the body rather than their relative importance). We will not deal here with these minor chakras, but it is worth looking at your own body to see if you can find the location of any of these other centres.

If you run a finger against the palm of your other hand very lightly and gently you may be able to locate a point that seems to have the most energy. This is the location of a chakra within

179

your hand (equivalent to the base of spine chakra in the seven major chakras).

Or imagine what would happen if you were driving in a car, fairly fast but steadily and safely when suddenly a large lorry pulls out in front of you. What happens to your body? Most of us will feel a pain, a 'pull' or strong sensation of some kind in our belly or solar plexus area. This is the contraction of the chakra located at that point.

The major chakras may be seen as 'rotating discs' that, on the level of the subtle body, are attached to the spine at seven specific points, from the base of the spine up to the very top. The following descriptions of the chakras are meant to be suggestive and should be read with constant reference to the diagram. We will look first at the chakras that have an 'internal duality', that is they are involved with inner balance, then those whose 'duality is external', that is, are involved with the balance between the individual and his or her environment.

THE BELLY CENTRE (MANIPURA CHAKRA)

The belly chakra is dual in nature since the left and right-hand sides of the individual have to be balanced for it to be effectively and fully open. In other words, if mind and feelings are not balanced there will be distortions of manipura energy.

This chakra is also often associated with the solar plexus. You can consciously radiate energy out from your solar plexus. When you do, notice how people will start to treat you differently. If you see someone as a 'bad' person in some way they will be just that; on the other hand, if you radiate energy as light from your solar plexus, and you do not see that person in a negative light, then they are free – and you are, too.

THE MIDHEAD CENTRE (AJNA CHAKRA)

This chakra is also dual in nature but on a higher or deeper level. Balance of the left-hand and right-hand energies is again necessary for its full opening, which represents 'love under will' in its clearest aspect.

Closely associated with the pineal gland, the 'ajna' centre is not between the eyebrows, as often quoted, being the 'third eye', but is situated in the centre of the cranium.

When you tune into and open your midhead chakra, you experience life as if you are the cause of everything in your universe.

THE HEART CENTRE (ANAHATA CHAKRA)

The heart chakra has a dual nature 'hidden behind it'; this can be understood through the archetypes of Love and Will. The heart chakra is really a trinity. The belly and midhead chakras will function even if there is not balance, albeit in a distorted fashion. The heart chakra is more of an 'on–off affair – it is open if there is balanced energy between Love and Will, closed if there is not.

If a heart is totally closed and never opens, it leads to heart-death through it becoming clogged up or blocked, unable to allow the free passage of energy. If a heart is totally open, and never able to close even when appropriate, it leads to heart-death in the form of heart attack (heart pumping too fast, blow-out). A connected and subtly effective heart chooses to open or close as appropriate to the situation at hand, being able to heal itself and others, but also able to protect its body, its means of expression. To tell how open a heart is, ask it how much compassion does it have, ask it about values, and feel its level of spiritual love.

The heart is associated with 'higher' feelings, values, love, service, altruism, and so on. Humanity as a whole is said to be moving, in the current age, from a primary focus on solar plexus issues towards a new connection and awakening of the heart values.

Relax and centre.

Let yourself become very still. Move your consciousness to your heart, put your awareness there, and for a while just feel its energy, both on physical and more subtle levels. Ask your heart for a symbol that represents its energies. Let this symbol emerge in your consciousness – do not censor or judge your symbol, but trust in your heart's wisdom. Whatever your symbol is, talk to it, ask it questions and listen to anything it may have to tell you. This may involve a verbal dialogue, or the symbol may simply change in size or brightness.

Imagine a single, powerful ray of sunshine shines on to your symbol, really charging it up, strengthening and brightening it. Strongly feel your connection with this symbol.

In your own time, come back to ordinary consciousness and write about your exchange with your heart symbol, the image (you may want to draw it), and about your relationship with your heart.

THE THROAT CENTRE (VISUDDHI CHAKRA)

The throat chakra only opens when the heart chakra is open, and it has to be open for energy to be channelled effectively and fully to the midhead and crown chakras.

The throat is about a whole range of expression, from physical expression through psychic communication to the true speaking of spirit from and through the heart. To see if a throat centre is open ask how effective the person is in the world, in their chosen field, how influential, and how able to express him or herself clearly?

THE BASE OF SPINE, GENITAL AND TOP OF HEAD CENTRES (MULADHARA, SVADISTHANA, SAHASARA CHAKRAS)

These three chakras are apparently, within the functioning of the individual, single in nature. But these, too, have a dual nature. Whereas with the other chakras the concern is with inner balance, these three chakras are concerned with outer balance. Muladhara – survival in the world; svadisthana – interplay and interpersonal relationships, particularly sexually oriented; and sahasara – the realisation of unity within and without, and the connection to the universal. The visuddhi chakra is also involved with outer balance – the outer, creative aspect of harmony and balance within.

It is interesting to look at the dynamic between the three lowest chakras, the base of spine, sexual and solar plexus centres. Males often make a strong connection between the base of spine and sexual chakras, connecting power with sexuality. Women, on the other hand, tend to connect the base of spine centre more strongly with the solar plexus. Whether, in both cases, this is because of conditioning or is genetic is not certain. It leads to confusion, however, when these centres are not properly functioning, which is the case with the majority of people. It is as if we divert the energy required for the proper functioning of the three grounding energy centres into building our walls of protection and separation.

Because of this connection, men tend to express their power distortions through their sexuality, whereas women tend to do so through their emotions.

With each of the following descriptions, vividly visualise and feel the energy described for each chakra location:

- *Sahasara* Blood pulses in the brain, at the very top of the skull; draw all your body forces there.
- *Ajna* There are pulsations in the brain, behind the frontal bone in the middle of the forehead.
- *Visuddhi* Concentrating on the region of the throat, imagine the sound of 'u' (as the middle latter of a-u-m) there.
- *Anahata* Concentrate on the heart, perceive your heart-beats. Imagine the blood circulation throughout the whole body.
- *Manipura* In the area between the solar plexus and the navel, perceive blood pulsations. Imagine the energy of assimilation.
- *Svadisthana* Contract your perineum, then concentrate on the sensations perceived between your lower belly and the base of your penis or clitoris. Imagine sexual dynamism.
- *Muladhara* Concentrate on the zone activated by contraction of the anus and perineum. Imagine the life energy that informs the human species, particularly you as a manifest individual.

The following exercise is a sample one for contacting any of the chakras. Incorporating the above instructions will help to enrich your experience.

Relax and centre.

Tune into your body and receptively allow one chakra to call your attention, to 'make itself heard' so to speak. Alternatively choose the chakra you wish to contact and concentrate your energy there.

Give a voice to this chakra. Allow it to speak to you. Listen to what it has to say.

Engage in active dialogue with the chakra, using discrimination about what it says.

Ask it about its relationship with the other chakras, particularly the ones directly above and below it.

Ask it about itself and particularly its *purpose* in this life.

Thank the chakra, and ask it to continue to perform effectively for you in this life.

Write about your experience immediately in your diary.

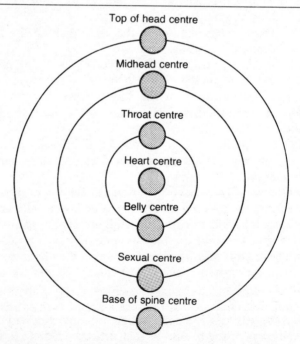

Figure 8: The Circle of Energies

As figure 8 shows, the upper and lower chakras connect to each other and they all revolve around the heart, at the centre of the system. The occult adage 'as above so below' is well exemplified by this, with the crown chakra, for example, connecting to the base chakra in a clearly harmonious way. The diagram shows the uniting of the macrocosm with the microcosm, the condition achieved when the heart is truly open. The personality revolves around its central core identity, and the soul is clearly heard, seen and felt in the person's life.

It is interesting, as shown in the diagram of the Caduceus, or Staff of Mercury, that this image, associated with healing, again corresponds with the chakras and the human body.

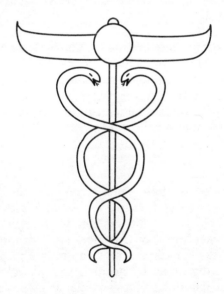

Figure 9: The Staff of Mercury

The staff is equivalent to the spine which is called shushumna in the original chakra system. The two serpents then correspond to Ida and Pingala, energies representing the left and right sides of our make-up, or our connections to the male and female polarities of energy. When these two energies are balanced, the central channel (shushumna, the subtle spine) opens and the kundalini inspiration may rise, charging up and clearly opening all the chakras up to the level attainable by the individual in his or her present state of incarnation.

Relax and centre.

Take a few deep breaths, then tune into your body. Receptively allow one chakra to call your attention, to make itself heard. You can give it a voice, and hear what it has to tell you about your energy on that level. Using discrimination about what it says, use this information to help you get a better and clearer connection to that level of energy within your total system.

You may want to check out the relation between this chakra and other chakras, particularly those directly above and below it. Are these relations harmonious, or are there issues that you can help resolve? What does this relationship between the chakras actually mean in your life – what can you change so that it improves?

At another time use these same techniques for investigating other people, maybe your clients if you work with individuals, or members of your family or friends. Imagine seeing the person's chakras, and look for blockages, distortions in the energy, patches of darkness or brightness and so on. Look for where attention may be needed, and try to visualise the desired moves. Do not be judgemental at all in anything you see, and do not share anything negative with another person. To use subtle energies effectively you need to be subtle on an intellectual level too.

· 14 ·

PERSON TO PERSON
Exploring Expression

Love one another, but make not a bond of love:
Let it rather be a moving sea between the shores of your
souls.
Fill each other's cup but drink not from one cup.
Give one another of your bread but eat not from the same
loaf.
Sing and dance together and be joyous, but let each of you
be alone.
Even as the strings of a lute are alone though they quiver
with the same music. . .
Give your hearts, but not into each other's keeping.
For only the hand of Life can contain your hearts.
And stand together yet not too near together:
For the pillars of the temple stand apart.
And the oak tree and the cypress grow not in each other's
shadow.

KAHLIL GIBRAN

If we keep everything we do to ourselves, if we shut off our
energy from other people, we may grow individually but we will
deny ourselves the joy of interaction. To express your sensing,
your feeling or your thinking is to take a risk – you may be
rejected or shunned, ridiculed or ignored. On the other hand,
not to express yourself is to take the greater risk of living in
isolation, cut off from your fellow creatures, 'dead' to the full
gamut of happiness and sorrow that you are able to experience
in your life.

We will explore some aspects of interpersonal relating, but
really everything we do in life can be seen within this arena,

for we are not isolated islands but rather we are part of one body of existence. There are times when it is appropriate to keep yourself to yourself, to be silent and not to share your energies. Honour your inner wisdom when such times occur in your life, and respect your act of silence. At other times, be willing to explore who you are and what you do as it relates to other people, other places and other beings of whatever kind. In this chapter we will look at a few ways to facilitate this process, but the only way you can truly explore your expression is through expressing yourself and the reactions in both yourself and others when you did this.

The following exercise will help you look in depth at some of the major relationships in your life.

Relax and centre.

Using a large piece of paper, draw a circle in the middle of it, quarter the rest of the space and put the names of four people with whom you are currently involved at the corners of the four boxes. Using the circle at the middle as a focus, tune into your centre and clearly self-identify. Then choose one of the four people and do a free drawing in their 'box' to represent the relationship, not just the person (in other words, do not just draw a representation of the person, but tune into what the interaction between you feels like and try to represent this in your drawing). You can do this with a pencil, colours and make it as complicated or as simple as you wish; the important thing is to get down a representation of the current state of your relationship with this person.

When you are ready, tune back to your centre (the circle in the middle), then choose to go into another box and do a drawing for the relationship with that person. Repeat the process until you have a drawing in all four boxes. If you do not have time to complete this part of the exercise in one go, it is all right to leave the drawing and come back at another time.

When you have four drawings, spend some time tuning into your centre before continuing the exercise. When you feel centred, look at the four relationships and see what differences you can find in the drawings, what common elements there are (look for colour, shading broken or unbroken lines, shapes and patterns as well as what is more obviously depicted in the actual shapes drawn).

We live in a world of mirrors wherein what I imagine I sense or feel is really a reflection or image of myself. When I see you I see an image of myself, and when you see me it is an image of you. We are fully responsible for how we create our world. Wilson Van Dusen described this succinctly: 'I am not only my brother's keeper. . . I am my brother.'

The ideas and images we have about other people and other things tend (consciously or unconsciously) to get projected or radiated out on to the other people or the world. This energy is then attracted back to us. We are not helpless victims (even when things 'happen to us'), we create our own reality.

It is so important to make a clear discrimination between experience and expression. We often believe something is not complete unless it has been expressed, whereas sometimes experiencing is all that is necessary. When expression is appropriate it should come from a direct experience, not just from a fantasy, unless it is clearly defined as such. To say 'I feel bad when you pick your nose' is not owning one's own experience. How can someone else picking their nose actually make you feel 'bad'? It cannot be over-emphasised that the only person you have to work on is yourself.

Look around your room and, picking any object, say 'I see (whatever it is), I imagine (whatever), I feel (whatever)'. For example, 'I see paper with writing on it, I imagine it's a finished chapter of this book, I feel contented. I see a stain on the carpet, I imagine it's spilt tea, I feel annoyed.'
Take your time and, being honest with yourself for each element of the formula, repeat this several times with

different objects. Notice the differences between what you actually, directly perceive, what you actually, directly feel, and the fantasies in between. This is how we normally operate in the world, interpreting all our experiences (from outside or inside) through a set of fantasies and belief-structures.

After you have practised this exercise a few times, try doing it with another person, taking it in turns to say I see, I imagine, I feel, while looking at the other person. Notice how an imaginary wall prevents direct contact.

Often we do not express all we wish to; we start the expression, then, depending upon the reaction to it, we may stop altogether, suppress elements of it, or divert into something else. It is a major principle of interpersonal relationships that we need to express 'what is', without judgement or censorship. When we do this we open up the possibility of change.

If you want someone to stop seeing you in a certain way you have to stop seeing them in a certain way. It is so easy to say 'you should be like me, you should do what I do,' instead of accepting others as they are. We see people in 'boxes' and relate to the box instead of the person. Then if I put you in a box, I'm in a box as well. So we do not have to be there, do not have to take real risks in opening up, and can act as if there is 'nobody home'. Of course, fortunately, the converse is true, too – if I see you as okay then I am okay too.

When you find it difficult to accept others as they are, it is useful to ask yourself: 'What is it in me that is stopping me accepting you as you are?', and 'How is this other person serving me?'

Sometimes we feel we should not be demanding, should give the other person more space, more love, or whatever. While this may be – and is often – true, it is also important to be aware of our own needs. It is often useful to make a demand and be willing to have yes or no as the answer. People tend to match our expectations – if we decide another person is going to say no then they will tend to do just that. People accommodate us, which is why it is so easy to label someone as something and find evidence for its validity. It is also true, however, that we get what we put out – so the more we label others the more we become labelled ourselves.

We have to acknowledge the other person as being who they are and having what they have, and to be willing for change to happen in the relations between us. This is not so easy, but at least through trying we can move ourselves forward in a positive direction. To be loved, the only thing you have to give up is the experience of not being loved. If you can believe or imagine it is possible, it is, otherwise it is not possible and there is no way it will happen.

We are great mirrors of each other, great teachers to each other, and we can use that . . . we love to mirror off each other. Let that mirroring become of the highest octave so that as you look out of yourself . . . you see the wholeness of that other being.

CHRIS GRISCOM

The primary way of honouring another person is through honouring yourself. You have to give them the right to be, to grumble and moan if that is what they need to do, to give them the space for whatever they need. For a relationship to be really working, the other person or people in it have to be willing to do the same.

Some actions you can take to honour someone else with whom you are in a relationship, include:

- appreciating the differences between you;
- giving them positive feedback when they make acts which honour you;
- acknowledge clearly what you appreciate in them;
- treat the problems which arise between you as blessings which give you the opportunity to grow;
- recognise and worship the god or goddess within them.

You have to accept who they are, even if you do not accept what they do, and make this explicit through saying, in some form or another: 'I accept who you are but I don't like you doing "whatever". For me, this is what you do, not what you are.' If something is not to your liking, can you really blame anyone else but yourself, and even if you feel you can, is blaming someone a truly positive way forward, or just a way of putting another wall between you and the other person?

The 'Gestalt Prayer', devised by Fritz Perls, is most useful. Say the following few lines to your partner while he or she repeats each line back to you. Be aware of what you are saying.

'I am I;
You are you;
I am not in this world to live up to your expectations;
You are not in this world to live up to my expectations;
I am I;
You are you;
If we meet that is great;
If we do not meet, that is okay too.'

Set and Setting

In an individual person, the 'set' is everything you are inside, your feelings, emotions, thoughts, ideas, memories, imaginings, and so on. The 'setting' is the place where you are, the outside environment. The same is true for a relationship, the set being the collective totality of the two or more persons involved. The set and setting of a relationship has to do with the relationship seen as a whole, as an entity in its own right. It could be described as the existential reality of the relationship. It has a tendency to appear constant in an overall sense, though it is usually changing under the surface at all times.

Not all relating happens within a wider context, of course, for much of our relating happens in a simple 'here and now' way, directly concerned with the situation at hand just as it is happening. This occurs more in terms of the environment, the setting, what is going on in the very moment-to-moment passage of time we call 'now'. Such relating has a tendency to be constantly changing, though under the surface there will be hidden consistencies, based on the walls and other blocking patterns within the personality.

Neither form of relating is better than the other. The key is to be able to have both and apply them as appropriate to the situation with each person you relate to, whether on a long or short-term basis.

Roles and Relationships

There are basic ways in which people play manipulative roles within a relationship. These roles occur singly or in combination within the different subpersonalities in each of us. They can be described as:

- the placating type: smoothing over differences, being nice, covering up, saying 'it's not so bad really, we'll get over it'.

- the avoiding type: being quiet, pretending not to understand, changing the subject, playing helpless, saying 'I can't help it, I don't hear you'.

- the blaming type: judging, bullying, complaining, saying 'it's always your fault, why don't you do something about it'.

- the preaching type: lecturing, explaining how they're right, calculating, saying 'so and so says. . ., you should. . ., what you are really doing is. . .'

The important thing is not to be looking for these types in others for judgemental or any other reasons, but to be looking for them within oneself. Then the walled energy can be reintegrated and used positively.

There are four basic principles for ideal relationships, to make our living as free as that described by Gibran at the beginning of this chapter. If you do not recall the quote, reread it now before continuing. Even if you do remember it, it is always worth rereading!

1. I come to you as a whole, both of us are whole; we both have needs outside the relationship.

2. I give you space and freedom; I love you unconditionally.

3. I love you from my being which is not deficient; I will own my shadow, and not project it on to you.

4. Whatever is going on I still want what is right for you; I support you even though I do not like it. I am willing to surrender to how our relationship evolves.

The following is an exercise you may like to do with someone
you know, or, if you prefer, it is possible to do it alone by
imagining the other person. It is most effective if done with
another, however.

Sit face to face and decide who goes first. Each of you will
perform the following, taking each section at a time.

Say out loud: 'This person has problems.' Look at the other
person and see them as having problems. If you imagine
you know what they are, you can make these problems
explicit.

Say out loud: 'This person is a soul who has chosen obstacles
to help them grow.' Look at the other person and see them
as a soul.

Say out loud: 'This person is both the self and a personality.'
Realise the truth of this statement.

---

*When you've said all of the bad things and all of the good things
you haven't been saying, you'll find that what you've really
been withholding is 'I love you'. You don't have to go looking
for love when love is where you came from.*

ROBERTO ASSAGIOLI

The different ways we relate with others can also be described
as falling into four groups.

1.   Relating primarily on an unconscious level, usually in
a way that is very dependent upon sexual contact. There is
not much contact on an everyday conscious level, not much
understanding or empathy.

2.   Relating primarily on a spiritual level, as spirit to spirit.
This includes many so-called 'platonic' relationships and

will tend to be very heady, and to deny sensation-based aspects of interrelating. It is 'friendship only'.

3.   Relating primarily in a personality to personality way, tending to keep things light and loose, but unfortunately also never becoming very deep or inspiring.

4.   Relating primarily in a holistic way, involving all parts of the personality, including the darker parts, and all levels of the being including the soul and the self. This ideal can be experienced at times in all relationships, but for it to become the primary focus there is a need for much work to be done. It is a process of evolution, it will not just happen.

Family Relating

It is useful to distinguish what actually happened in our primary relationship (our family with our parents or guardians) from what we imagine happened or simply believe without consideration. Answer the following questions as truthfully as you are able. They will help you to find the truth of your family relating and learning.

What skills did you learn from your family that are useful to you as an adult?

What would it be better for you to change to become more effective as an adult?

What role models did you have in your family that aid you now?

And what role models from your family hinder you now?

What roles did you play in your family that have meaning for you now (for example hero, peacemaker, troublemaker, joker, etc.)?

Which of these roles are you stuck with and would do well to change?

> Close your eyes and allow a symbol to emerge that repre-
> sents your primary family relationship. What meaning can
> you find in that symbol today?
> Think of your family as chosen by you, having given you
> exactly what you needed.

After considering these eight points, answer the following
question in the light of your new knowledge: What is my
purpose in life?

Our primary relationship forms the basis of all our future
relating. Emotional patterns are transformed from parental
relationships to personal ones. Perhaps your mother or father
exhibited over-development of their maternal or paternal roles,
'mollycoddling' and being over-protective, or at the other
extreme, being overstrict and restrictive; do you follow this
pattern? Perhaps your parents were prone to do their living
through others (particularly their children – you). Do you
repeat this pattern? Perhaps within you there is an over-
development of romance and/or sex? Where did you get this
from? Perhaps you are resisting your own maternal or paternal
instincts because you are resisting what you learned about
them through your parents; on the other hand, perhaps you
are over-attached to these instincts through over-identification
with your parents.

We learn the ways we relate to the Love and Will archetypes
from our parents. If our relationship with Love and Will is
clearly formed, then we know it is okay to be ourselves (love
ourselves) and it is okay to change (will or empower ourselves).
If these relationships are not so clearly defined, and in most of
us this is exactly the case, then we exhibit the corresponding
distortions. It is important to remember, however, that we are
not victims to our parents – the Love and Will archetypes were
working through them, too.

We have no moral right to change our 'real, out there' parents
in any way, but we can do what we like with our 'inner parents'.
Our relationship to Love and Will does change anyway, so why
not consciously change our inner parents? Imagine the parents
you feel would be perfect for you, then replace the old images
with these new ones. If you repeat it often enough, the energies

of Love and Will can transfer to these new images and come through in a less distorted way.

On the other hand, perhaps it is best not to interfere with the way your soul has chosen the parents for you, and what you have to learn from them. In this case why not dialogue with the guardian angel of each of your parents to learn about them on this deeper level, and to discover more about your relationship to them? Whether you choose either or both of these programs is up to you; take care to choose as is appropriate to where you are in your process, and your connection to your Purpose in life.

You can go further than your parents ever could in your relationship to the archetypes of Love and Will. What did they teach you about these energies? You are the cause of your learning, not your parents. Recall what has been said already about victim consciousness and apply this knowledge to your understanding of your relationship with your parents. A victim is powerless; you are not. You have the choice – to be a victim or not, to take responsibility for who you are, to realise that, whatever situation you are in, you created it just that way for your learning.

It is always true that, whatever we do it is the best we can do at that time. This is also always true of others, including our parents and our partners. Realising this brings acceptance, and true acceptance brings a clarity to our ability to be ourselves, able to love or will as appropriate.

Bless your parents for doing the best they could. Bless your partner for doing the best he or she is able. Bless yourself for doing the best you can.

Forgiveness removes any lack of wholeness. Forgiveness brings love – both to the person forgiven and to the forgiver. You can never have enough forgiveness.

Personal Reality

You carry your mother and father within you, and much of your relating is a mirror of their ways of teaching you to relate, and their relating to you. You need to own who you are, and your own ways of relating.

Our personal reality is a combination of projection and perception. What you have to work on in any relationship is your perceptual reality. For any relationship to happen it takes at least two, but it only takes one person to change the game. All you can do anyway is work on your end of it, you create and live your own reality. If you stop projecting your 'stuff' and own who you are, and who the other person is, then you start to get what you are putting out, and you can express yourself clearly and hear the expression of the other person clearly too. Remember, there is no blame.

Relax and centre.

Imagine yourself in a difficult situation with another person. Take some time really to picture and feel this situation, either real or imaginary.

Then imagine yourself 'out there', as it were, actually in the other person. See the situation from their viewpoint.

Come back to yourself and then gradually imagine you toss the 'you out there' a rope, lassoing your consciousness, and slowly bringing it back to the centre of your body. Really feel this happening as you do it.

Be yourself. Let others be themselves.

Sexual Relating

To understand the sexual component in any relationship, we need to explore the meaning and intention within the relationship. To isolate sex is not the most effective way to do this; we should rather see it as part of the whole picture. All our walls and negative patterns – for example, our resistance to the self, our identifications, our fears and so on, all are played out in sexual relating. It is very rare for it to be a pure biological act, for it always involves feelings, emotions, thoughts, fantasies and so on.

Sex is often used as means to a different end than its obvious own end – it can be used to avoid difficulties, to avoid boredom, to overcome other difficulties in the relationship, as a form of 'vampirism', to have power over the other person, and so on. On the other hand, sex can be viewed as spiritual, as a holy act of union between people. When one and one come together sex does not give us two, it gives us a newly formed, ecstatic one again. Our inner desire for unity can be met and fulfilled through a positive attitude towards sex, and all the principles described in this chapter for good interpersonal relations can be applied to sex.

Tantric and other sexual magickal practices can allow us to be ourselves in a new, exciting way. If you reread Chapter 8 on the body, and apply the breathing techniques described there, along with the suggestions for sexual relating, you will be using the methods of tantra in your life. The most important part of these techniques is in bringing awareness to play in your sexual life, then applying the principles you have learned for improving your own life, that of your partner, and then that of the planet as a whole. Awareness in sex brings vast amounts of energy for you to use in whatever way seems appropriate to you at the time. Use it wisely and the energy will continue to increase, enabling you to fulfil your purpose more effectively.

Most sexual problems fall into either or both of these categories: not operating sexually (too little), and only operating sexually (too much).

Relax and centre.

Visualise a door with the word 'sexuality' on it. Imagine yourself opening this door and looking through to see what is on the other side. View what is there in detail. If you feel willing to do so, step into this other world and explore what is there. It is the realm of your own sexuality.

When you are ready, come back from this vision and distinctly and firmly close the door shut behind you. Return to your ordinary consciousness.

Consider what you saw in your vision of sexuality. Consider what your other senses told you about this place, and how you felt there. Look for the qualities present behind the forms you saw. Look for aspects of union. Did you see emotional patterns reflected in your vision? How is your self-image reflected there, did you identify with what you saw, and are you able to dis-identify from it?

What is the meaning you put on your sexuality? What are your attitudes and concepts about your sex? Consider how you have been conditioned about sex.

Interpersonal Expression

The exploration of our interpersonal expression is perhaps the most exciting aspect of our existence in this life for it gives us the opportunity to know ourselves not only singly, as ourselves, but in combination with other people. However you relate to other individuals, whether your relationships are comparatively balanced or are in conflict, it is worth remembering that at all times we are all equal souls learning to grow and manifest in our earthly existence. The following exercise helps to make such a connection.

Relax and centre.

Imagine each individual in your current awareness as a point of light, a source of love, life and liberty.

Extend this awareness to all the beings on the planet earth.

Imagine this same awareness in every other person; see yourself as connected to an interrelated grid. We are all connected like spokes of a wheel to one central point of light. See this in your vision.

Contact that point of light and realise both your uniqueness
and your totally interdependent connection.

You are both alone, unique and individual, and together,
connected and at one.

· 15 ·

COLLECTIVE CONSCIOUSNESS
Exploring Integration

We are planetary people, sharing in the responsibility of caring for a world that up to now has mostly cared for us. Innocence is sacrificed in our exponential growth of responsibility. What we do makes a profound difference.

JEAN HOUSTON

It is so important to realise that what we do makes a profound difference, when so often we can be convinced both by our own inner feelings of inadequacy and by the turn of events outside of us, that we are bound to a world that we, as individuals, cannot affect or change in any way. Yet at those times when we feel connected, when we are whole, when we are soul with personality, we understand we are a collective consciousness, connected to absolutely everything else. Every act we make does have an effect, although it may be so small we hardly notice it ourselves, let alone believe it could have any effect on the planet or even the universe.

Sometimes when we are identified, we interpret our experience in terms of separation, alienation, loneliness and fear. We 'imagine' there is an inseparable gulf between us and the rest of the world. We may even feel unworthy, as if others really knew us, and what is in our hearts, they would reject us in some way. This wall is very insidious because it can look like a simple psychological matter whereas it is a subtle transpersonal avoidance. In fact, if we could see into other people from the level of the soul we would see that they are the same as us. We would know that the gulf that we had previously imagined was between us is illusionary. We can find the strength to do this from living our lives as we truly choose to do. This is real freedom, to be honest to one's inner wisdom and connectedness and to act upon it without effort or distinction.

We are the same, not just humans, but all life forms are the same in that they are part of the interconnected web of life. We are often in a state where we appear to be separate, indeed many of us may live our whole lives in such a state, but all those who have ventured forth into the realms of individual exploration testify to such a connection.

Collective Consciousness

The notion of a collective consciousness is not new, and is undoubtedly proven to all those who have ever attuned themselves to their process and had realisations, synchronistic happenings, insights into the working of the unconscious and affirming incidents. The collective consciousness is the light of which the collective unconscious is the shadow. Both are necessary parts of the whole person, and while we need to investigate the collective unconscious, and be receptive to it, we also need to open up to and sense the collective consciousness. It is a web of interrelated and interconnected life, living energy that permeates every material thing. It includes those things vibrating at such a slow rate that we do not see their life energy (for example, rocks). It includes all the different vibrations of life forms within our range of sensing (from single-cell beings through plants to mammals including humans). It includes those 'entities' which we can sense at the edge of our awareness, and more and more so as the New Age manifests – the life forms to which we give names like 'planets' and 'galaxies'. It also includes energy forms that vibrate at such fast rates that they are invisible to us. There are innumerable vibratory levels, inhabited by all sorts of creatures, some of which are given names like extraterrestrials, or archangels, or gods and goddesses.

Let go of your linear sight, and hear where you are, here where you are. Encompass the fullness around you and in this fullness is fulfilment. Be the centre of your energy and literally see what I say. Be with me now on this voyage of discovery within the collective consciousness. Take joy in your abundance and pleasure in your freedom.

COMMUNICATION 1986

When we feel separate we experience loneliness, and yet even in this we can find connections with the collective consciousness. Robert had such an experience: 'It was as if the uniqueness and individual experience of me came down to loneliness. I almost started panicking, ringing people up, catching trains to go and see people, anything to fill the space, but I somehow knew this was not the way. It was not wrong but I felt I had to go through the experience, grow through it. I went out to the park where I enjoyed nature and being and being me. And now I am back home sitting writing this and the intensity of the loneliness is coupled with a realisation: I can enjoy being alone, for that is where I am, and at the same time I am not alone because I am connected to everyone and everything else; the bird on the lake, the rose in the flower bed, the ice-cream wrapper on the path, all I saw, I see, and sense in every way is me and I am it for we are all part of the one total beingness of the planet earth. We are in no way separate.'

When Robert says he can enjoy being alone, he is talking from an aspect of his personality. At the same time, he is realising the truth behind this on the soul level. Having touched the soul, he then connects, with this same knowledge, to the collective consciousness.

Relax and centre.

Imagine you are standing on an open plain. It is night time, and the sky is clear. Above and around you are a myriad of stars in a perfectly clear sky. Look at the magnitude of the sky for a while.

Imagine your consciousness goes out to a star. Be a star in the heavens. As this star, see the planets, meteorites, moons and anything else that might be in your 'stellar system'. Be aware of these objects surrounding you and orbiting around you. Take some time to really imagine yourself as this star.

Now look further out and see other stars all around you, the other stars within your galaxy. Look further out and see other galaxies, see space filled with stars and galaxies in every direction.

Imagine your consciousness goes out to one of these stars in one of these galaxies. Become that star . . . and, again, see the planets that orbit you as you fly through space at almost unimaginable speed. Look further afield and see the stars and galaxies that surround you . . .

Now realise that all the stars in all the galaxies are interconnected, are all part of one heaven. Realise your insignificant, yet, at the same time, vital place within your universe.

This is the same for all living things on the planet earth – each of us are connected and part of one living body of consciousness. It is said that only humans beings forget this.

The Soul Rays

There are eight main ways to spiritual realisation, although these ways are not sharply divided and, in fact, frequently overlap. Each of these ways is associated with a particular Soul Ray which emanates from the Universal Spirit. In other words, each individual soul is 'charged with' or 'informed by' the energy of one or more of these Soul Rays. Each of us has one or more of these rays manifesting through different aspects of our being. In essence (on the level of the spirit) we are connected to all eight of the rays, but in terms of our soul and personality some of these rays become foreground to our particular stage of evolution.

Name of Ray	Number	Alternative Name
WILL	1	Power
LOVE	2	Wisdom
ACTIVITY	3	Action
BEAUTY	4	Harmony
KNOWLEDGE	5	Science
DEVOTION	6	Idealism
RITUAL	7	Organisation
TRANSCENDENCE	8	Immanence

Most people have two primary influences, one for the soul and one for the personality. Then, within the personality, one ray will be found particularly to influence the mind, another the feelings, and a third the body and senses. When looking for the influence of these rays within yourself or anyone else, it is important not to be dogmatic. The divisions between the rays are not clear cut, and it is often difficult to tease out the difference between the influence various rays have on different parts of the person.

The 'height' of the ray is how it manifests in its 'pure' form; the 'depth' of the ray is, to a greater or lesser degree, how it manifests through the personality. The task, once a ray's influence has been identified, whether in its 'height' or 'depth', is to elevate it. This means to use techniques to create dynamic balance between the various components involved in the manifestation of that ray. This might take the form of personality work, meditation and/or visualisation; always, however, it will involve a deep-rooted connection with soul energy through self-identification exercises.

There now follows a description of the individual rays. The exercises described after all the rays can usefully be performed by everyone, as they have intrinsic value as exercises separate from their connection to any particular ray. They will also help you realise the power of all the rays within yourself.

THE RAY OF WILL

This ray is less common than the other rays. Called 'the heroic way', it is the way of leaders, for 'good' or 'bad'. This ray is wilful, one-pointed, quick to action, prompt, decisive, competitive, and has the power of physical endurance. People on this ray tend to judge emotions as negative. If distorted they are self-centred and isolated, assertive in a judgemental way, and even violently psychopathic.

Their task is to temper their will with love; to become more understanding and co-operative, to build as well as to destroy, and to align their personal will with their true Purpose.

Relax and centre.

Imagine you are in your meadow. You are holding a magickal wand. Visualise the kind of wand you would most like to have.

Taking the time to ground yourself as you walk, go up your mountain until you reach the top. Hold the wand in the air, and visualise a beam of light from the sun striking the wand and energising it in a new, more powerful way. Perhaps the wand will change form, or shape, size or kind, perhaps it will simply become brighter and more powerful.

When you are ready, bring your wand back to the meadow. Realise you can use your wand to make acts of will that further your personal development. Your wand, representing your will, through being energised by a transpersonal energy, is now stronger and more capable. Use it wisely.

THE RAY OF LOVE

Love permeates all things, and the Ray of Love is particularly difficult to separate from the other rays, yet it is a very specific path. People on this ray tend to be 'servers' to humanity, whether through medicine and healing, or in more indirect ways. It is the path of inclusiveness, of seeing the 'divine' in everything. Co-operation, brotherhood, and group consciousness are all important concepts to these people. Their purpose in life is to love and to ultimately transform individual love into Universal Love. The person on the Ray of Love will want to include as much as possible, and will realise him- or herself through relationships. They tend to be soft, sometimes to the point of inertia. If very distorted they become like a cushion that accepts all impressions, and holds the impression made by the last person to 'sit on them'. They are without boundaries.

Their task is enlarging and refining their overall positive attitude, and cultivating love in its pure form. They also need to learn to use their will more, to be courageous, to have direction, and to be able to say 'no'.

Relax and centre.

Make a list of four things you currently want. Be realistic but not limiting in your choice of these four 'wants'. Once you have chosen them, give them to yourself.

Now make a list of four things you can give. Again be realistic but not limiting in your choice of four things you can give. Once you have chosen them, do them – give them to people either literally or, if that is not possible, then symbolically.

THE RAY OF ACTION

For people of this type, there is no need for any ultimate goal, the going is sufficient in itself. They can be passionate and dispassionate at the same time. They can act on behalf of others with absolutely no self-interest. They are pragmatic and skilful, and deal with the element of earth very successfully. On the negative side they tend to be unconscious of deeper and higher feelings, so often are insensitive and/or manipulative and devious. They are very efficient and effective at getting a job done, but can get caught up in their activity and lose touch with its purpose.

Their task is to be still, to slow down, to allow 'being' as well as 'doing'. They need to cultivate Love, connect with their feelings, and develop aesthetic appreciation.

Relax and centre.

Choose three local places of interest – they could be museums, art galleries, castles, tumuli, standing stones, whatever – and make arrangements to visit each of them on three separate days. Keep to your decisions, and when at these places, slow down and let yourself have the time to really appreciate the beauty there. Particularly notice how being there makes you feel.

Then do the same again, but with three places you would *not* normally choose to visit.

THE RAY OF BEAUTY

'Harmony manifests as Beauty' is the watchword of this type. They are creative and intuitive people, and often have a deep understanding of both themselves and others. They see the divine in all forms, they can see true beauty in all manifestation. Ecstasy and agony are both familiar to these artistic types. On the negative side they find it difficult to make choices, and are easily spaced out (both in pleasant and unpleasant ways). Often they are adversely affected by other people's negative energies. They can be dreamy and impractical.

Their task is to cultivate persistence, and the will, particularly in self-assertion; also to connect with their creative impulses and manifest them in as pure a form as possible.

Find somewhere unobtrusive where you can sit and watch as many people as possible. You might choose, for example, a park bench or a seat in a shopping mall.

Relax and centre. Watch the other people as they pass by and consciously choose to see them all as beautiful. See each individual clearly and recognise the beauty which may manifest in an overall, total sense, in the way they walk or talk, in a particular feature, or shape of their body, or simply because they are alive. However it manifests, honour the truth of beauty. Be aware that all people have this beauty, not only those where you are, but everyone everywhere.

When you return home, stand naked before a mirror and see your beauty.

THE RAY OF SCIENCE

Using the mind, in both its abstract and concrete modes, with strong intuition and imagination, these types love exploring, and are often filled with waves of curiosity. Bright and clear of mind they can be tireless in the pursuit of knowledge. They tend, however, to be very out of touch with their emotional life, and are often stuck in mental identification. They can be excessively analytical, and opinionated, even arrogant about their beliefs. They are also insensitive to others.

Their task is to get in touch with their feelings, develop and appreciate their emotions. They need to balance their head and heart. They can also learn to use the mind to go beyond itself.

Relax and centre.

Imagine you are a scientist in a laboratory. On the bench in front of you is the most sophisticated computerised microscope that can see clearly and deeply into anything, whether it is manifest as form or is an unmanifest energy. Whatever you choose to put under the microscope appears on your computer screen.

Choose to look at your sensation body (etheric), then your feeling body (astral), then all your other bodies, physical and energetic, the parts of your personality – anything you choose. Allow whatever image(s) to emerge without judgement or censorship.

Your computerised microscope has further powers – when you change the image on the screen, it correspondingly changes whatever is under investigation. Use this function wisely and without fear to change what you see in appropriate ways.

THE RAY DEVOTION

This is the ray of mysticism, of devotion to a 'god', 'guru', ideal or cause. The devotion of this type is intense, and they are often completely dedicated to their work. They have a great urge for unity, and union with their desired transcendent goal. On the negative side they lack joy in their lives, and are overly serious. Often they do not see alternatives, and want to convert others to their 'one true' way. They include those who become harsh fanatics and 'fundamentalists'.

Their task is to enlarge themselves both mentally and emotionally, and refine their sense of devotion.

Relax and centre.

Imagine you have been invited to give a seasonal address on television that will be broadcast to all the people of all the nations of the earth. It will be translated word for word into every world language. The general theme is 'Devotion'.

Plan your address, and write it down, in a way that enlarges your understanding of devotion but which, at the same time, can be understood by everyone who hears it. Your message must be simple, and direct and speak of devotion in a way that is universally applicable to us all. It can be as long or as short as you like.

When you are ready, imagine you are making a video of your address. Using your written notes, read out your message clearly and distinctly, and with feeling. Enjoy the rapture of speaking to so many people, and respect the responsibility of this act.

THE RAY OF RITUAL

This is the ray of magick, of organising matter in such a way as to change consciousness, both on the inner and outer planes. People of this type tend to be organisers, making order out of chaos. They are in touch with Purpose and how to achieve that purpose. They are disciplined at their chosen creative tasks. Although not as inspired as the Beauty type they will usually get a lot more done. They give tremendous attention to detail, and are in touch with the rhythms of life. On the negative side they are often controlled by routines and their endless organisation can be boring both to themselves and others. They can also be rigid and, if given the opportunity, bureaucratic.

Their task is to develop their ritual, to put matter into rhythm, to give order to things that help people appreciate the rhythms and cycles of nature. Also they need to 'build a bridge' between their individual soul and the collective consciousness of spirit.

We will look at ritual in more depth in the next chapter, where its importance will be stressed. For now, look at the rituals you habitually perform in your daily life, and try to find ways to break out of the unconscious, unnecessary rituals, to refine and restructure the necessary ones, and to invent new ones that would enhance the quality of your life.

THE RAY OF TRANSCENDENCE

In previous Ages, only seven rays were usually described. In this New Age it appears that the Ray of Devotion is transforming into a 'new' ray, sometimes called 'The Ray of Transcendence'. It corresponds to the throat chakra, and thus is associated with clear soul expression, as opposed to the Ray of Devotion which is associated with the second chakra and limitation rather than inclusion. There is a direct link between these two chakras and a clear movement of energies between them.

This new ray, that is 'transcendent' in that it includes all the other rays, yet is more than them, could also be called the 'Ray of Immanence', as including all the other rays it also manifests them. Therefore it may be better to see it as an additional ray rather than a replacement for one of the old rays. Although we lose the magickal '7', it is replaced by an equally magickal '8', and we will be acting in an inclusive way that is truer to the new ray itself.

The Tasks of the Rays

There are tasks associated with all the rays. You will probably recognise some of yourself in all these types, but your task is to find which of these rays are those with which you particularly connect on the personality and on the soul levels.

For the personality ray, it is useful to ask yourself: From which ray do I live my everyday life? To find your soul ray ask yourself: Which ray do I experience during peak experiences?

When you have elucidated this, then you ask yourself these following questions for both the personality and soul rays:

What needs to be refined?
What needs to be elevated?

The previous sections on the individual rays should help you answer these last two questions.

Once you have found your 'rays' it is a useful exercise then to apply your knowledge of this system to other people; what rays do your parents, lovers, friends, colleagues, etc., operate from? What do they need to elevate and refine?

It is worth noting that whatever ray each of us follows we are all 'pilgrims' with the same goal, notwithstanding the difference of method. Through the diversity of the Eight Rays we make an approach to the essential divinity in us all, individually and collectively.

The Star of the Self

The following diagram shows 'The Star of the Self'. It shows the self at the centre of a six pointed star, and is an interesting meditation tool. As you look at it, see how the different polarities of, for example, will and love, are at opposite points on the star, while at the same time they are part of the same whole system, centred on a unique and individual self.

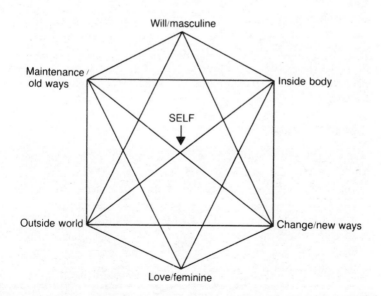

Figure 10: The Star of the Self

Meditation is of great value for connecting to the collective consciousness. When we meditate, in whatever way, we still ourselves inside, and, when stilled, we all are more connected both to our own inner source of energy and also to the collective consciousness through which we can channel universal energy.

Affirmations have a similar importance, and have the ability to connect us. Books on affirmations abound these days and are popular because the device of making affirmations is at the very least comforting (you can 'feel' like you have the ability to make a difference) and at the very best will bring about real change in a person's life.

Attunement to what is inside, to the soul, is the best way of connecting to the collective consciousness. Both meditation and affirmation are methods of attunement. Attunement is, simply, making a clear and conscious act that creates a connection to whatever it is you are attuning. You might simply subvocally voice your act of attunement, or you might construct a complicated ritual to ground this act in some way. You can attune at any time, but it is best to attune when you 'know' and 'feel' and 'sense' it is most appropriate to do so, when your energy is connected and powerful. You can also attune to physical locations, both while there, to help you connect and perhaps get a peak experience, and also to keep that connection to energy so you can choose, in imagination, to return there whenever you wish, whenever you need to reconnect to that particular energy.

Global Awareness

Our awareness is global. We are all part of an interconnected collective consciousness, a web of energy that connects everything to everything irrespective of time or place. On the level of the collective consciousness, you are no less connected to a distant star than you are to one of your toes. On the level of the collective consciousness, your knowledge and understanding of even one blazing atom of that distant star is no less than your knowledge and understanding of your own sensations.

To be connected in this way is not unusual, for everything and everyone is so connected. What is rare, at least amongst human beings (we cannot really speak of other entities or creatures), is to be conscious of this connection. To start moving in that direction, however, we can cultivate within ourselves what might be called 'global awareness'. This is a small piece of this total consciousness, the part associated with and involving our globe, the planet earth, and all the living creatures upon it. Many of the exercises in this book, and these last few chapters particularly, help us to move towards global awareness. To attain even moments of this connection is blissful, for we no longer experience ourselves as separate, lonely creatures awash in a sea of meaningless energies. We are connected, one with all our brothers, sisters, friends and relatives. We may choose to be alone but we can never be lonely.

True global awareness, like any other form of awareness, is only attained fully when it is put into action. We put global awareness into action through care for others, both those immediately within our field of awareness and activity, but also for all living and non-living things generally. We care for our environment, again locally and generally, and we make as many conscious acts as we can in order to further the cause of such care. There are as many different ways to contribute as there are people, but each of us, in our own way, can and will contribute to global awareness. Through making clear connections to the collective life force, we will transcend the current ills which threaten our whole family, from the lowliest single-cell creature to all the other life forms on our beautiful mother planet, including humankind.

EVOLUTION AND SYNTHESIS
Exploring The Future

At any moment we can let go of the resistance enough to draw light in, so that we can live fully – which is our birthright. Our birthright is to walk through walls, to raise the dead . . . it is to have the power, to have the wisdom to make the choice to live or die with grace.

CHRIS GRISCOM

We have four energies within us that correspond exactly with four primary energies that manifest in the world through the archetypes of Love, Life, Liberty and Light. These four energies are:

Love	genital energy (connected to substance and 'being')
Life	solar plexus energy (connected to awareness and consciousness of duality)
Liberty	heart energy (connected to individuation and becoming centred)
Light	integrated energy (connected to illumination and inspiration)

THE ENERGY OF LOVE

All division and duality is for the sake of love, to allow us the opportunity, from our separate existence, to form a union, to come together with another being and to be at one with him or her.

Love is the greatest healer, and being associated with our

genital energy is often expressed through that centre. Remember, however, as with all these qualities, although they have a primary level of focus, they can be expressed through all our centres. In the next exercise, you will be connecting love to your heart centre; after completing this exercise, try to find ways of connecting love to your genital, solar plexus and midhead energy centres.

Before continuing consider the question: What is love?

Start writing your answers to the question: What is love? On a piece of paper, continuing until you cannot think of any more answers. Do not censor or judge what responses come to you, ones that sound silly or off-mark can often give us the most interesting insights.

Relax and centre.

Imagine you have a crystal bowl on top of your head. Take some time to visualise this bowl clearly resting on your head. Feel its weight. Imagine all the ideas you have just had about love, all the words, thoughts, feelings, concepts – everything you 'know' about love is contained in this bowl. Vividly visualise all the words filling the bowl, and feel the extra weight they bring.

Now imagine a beam of sunlight strikes down into the contents of the bowl, and the words start evaporating. Picture this: the words melting and evaporating, and their remains drifting off into space. Continue this process until the bowl is empty, then continue the sunlight until the crystal bowl itself evaporates. Really feel its weight lifted from off your head.

The sunshine continues, and now the words and the bowl have gone, the light can now penetrate down through your body and right into your heart. Feel the energy beaming into your heart, and then, from there, circulating throughout your whole body, your whole being.

When all the words and concepts are gone you are left with the pure, unattached quality of love. Feel its presence within you. Do not think about it or do anything with this, just feel it and bask in its beauty and strengthening energy.

Return to your usual consciousness and ask yourself: In what ways can I express love in my life right now? Find at least one practical way in which you could express love in your life and then do it.

THE ENERGY OF LIFE

The energy of life is primarily experienced through our senses – not when we are interpreting what we experience, or thinking about it, or feeling it, or doing anything with it, but rather when we are just experiencing, just sensing.

In an earlier chapter you practised the awareness continuum, where you said 'Now I am aware . . .' and just let whatever comes up to be expressed. Do this again now for a while, alternating between inside and outside awareness. (For example: Now I am aware of a gurgling in my stomach, now I am aware of the colour of my keyboard, now I am aware of a slight ache in my neck, now I am aware of a phone ringing in the distance. . .)

What you experience inside yourself can be called your 'inner temple'; what you experience from outside are events in your 'outer temple'. These two 'temples' of experience are your territory for experiencing life. The distinction between the two is really an artificial one, for the inside and outside are part of one continuum. When you experience the two as one it brings a clear illumination, and strengthens the energy of the solar plexus.

We can use the technique of 'acting as if' as a central energiser for our solar plexus or life energy. You can 'act as if' anything you choose. Take some time now to try acting as if your inner temple and your outer temple are clearly and obviously connected. What does this experience feel like?

Relax and centre.

Close your eyes, be aware of whatever you experience there, then say to yourself: 'I am this inner temple.'

Then open your eyes and let your vision alight on whatever it chooses. Say to yourself: 'I am that outer temple.'

Continue this process, alternating between inside and outside, between saying 'I am this' and 'I am that'.

When you are contacting your inner space or temple in this way, you are aware of your body, feelings and thoughts without doing anything but affirming 'I am this'.

When you have your eyes open, looking into 'outer space', you are aware of your outer temple through your senses – what you see, hear, touch, taste or smell – without doing anything but affirming your experience, saying 'I am that'.

Realise this and that are identical.

Be aware that the 'I' which experiences the outside world and the 'I' which experiences the inside world are one, and you are able to choose whether to experience this, that or a combination of both.

THE ENERGY OF LIBERTY

The heart, the focus of the energy of liberty, acts as pivot between the microcosm (your inner temple) and the macrocosm (your outer temple). The sun, corresponding esoterically to the heart, is a similar pivot for the macrocosm. Thus the identity which is made between the two, gives meaning to the ancient occult adage 'as above, so below'.

When you are on the earth, experiencing terrestrial consciousness, you experience the sun as being born, increasing in strength to midday, decreasing in strength, then dying, disappearing, then being born again the next day. We 'know' this is not the truth, because, unlike our ancestors, we have the knowledge that the sun is central and the earth goes round it. The sun does not die. Yet, whatever we know, our experience in the most direct sense is no different from that of our ancestors.

Whatever you believe, whatever faith you hold, your experience of yourself as an individual soul is no different – you are born, increase, decrease, then die. Maybe you are born again, or go on to something else, depending upon your belief, but your experience at its simplest level is this cycle of birth and death.

If you could move your focus from the earth to the sun, you would now not experience the sun as dying and being reborn, instead you would experience the light as continuous, and see everything else revolving around you. If your awareness is centred on the sun, you have solar consciousness, and take quite a different perspective on life.

It is the same with the heart – if your focus moves to your heart, your 'inner sun' as it were, the place where you experience from the soul rather than the personality, then similarly you no longer see life and death in the same way, but rather experience a process of continuous love, life, liberty and light.

With the birth of this New Age, the consciousness of humankind is slowly changing in this way on a collective level. By the end of this age we will no longer be bound by terrestrial consciousness, but will be fully experiencing ourselves as solar beings. We will have stepped out of the old world into the new.

You can use your will to develop and evoke any desired soul quality, including liberty. The next exercise enables you to create inner and outer conditions through which you can connect with and nurture any desired quality – 'abstract' yet real, qualities such as love, joy, truth, beauty, strength, trust, and so on. The more frequently and regularly you perform it for any chosen quality, the stronger the quality becomes. You can use the exercise for any quality; here we will use it to connect with the quality of liberty.

Relax and centre.

Think about *liberty*. Hold the concept of liberty in your mind and reflect upon it. Ask yourself questions about this quality: What is it? What is its nature? What is its meaning? and so on. Record your ideas, and any images that emerge.

Be still and receptive; what does the quality mean to you now?

Realise the value of liberty, its purpose, its use in your life and on the planet as a whole. What differences would there be if liberty was in abundance?

Desire liberty.

Allow liberty to be in your body; assume a posture that expresses this quality. Relax all your tensions, let them drift away. Breathe slowly. Allow liberty to express itself on your face. Visualise yourself with that expression.

Evoke the quality of liberty. Imagine you are in a place where you feel liberty; a quiet beach, with a loved one, in a temple of liberty, wherever you choose. Try to really feel it. Repeat the word liberty several times. Let the quality permeate you, to the point of identification if possible. Allow yourself to be liberty.

Resolve to remain infused with liberty, to be the living embodiment of liberty, to radiate liberty.

Draw on a piece of paper or card the word liberty, using the colours and lettering that best convey the quality to you. Place this sign where you can see it daily, as often as possible. You can make several such signs and place them strategically around your home. Whenever you notice a sign, recall within yourself the feeling of liberty.

You can develop this exercise into a much more intense, prolonged ritual by performing it daily, and at the same time gathering together poetry, writings, pictures, symbols, artwork, dance, anything that symbolises for you your chosen quality. By surrounding yourself with these symbols, especially while performing the exercise, you can help deepen your sense of the quality. This is essentially identical with the use of correspondences in ritual magic.

If you find that attempting to evoke the desired quality brings the opposite (for example, if instead of liberty you get 'bondage', or, say, instead of joy you get sorrow), this is usually a sign that there is a wall of negative emotions stopping the development of the desired quality. If they are strong, stop the exercise and explore the negative feelings that are emerging, and without becoming entrapped in them, allow them to express themselves symbolically. Then let go of them and resume the exercise, realising that as you now evoke the quality it can fill the empty space left vacant by the released negative emotion.

Focus on the central truth that you have awareness, but you are not your awareness. This is true liberty.

THE ENERGY OF LIGHT

Light is illuminating, and our contacts with its energy are usually inspirational, often coming at unexpected moments in our lives. Fortunately, we can also connect with this light through the kind of exercises presented in this book, and through other similar techniques. Nothing helps us walk through walls better than the quality of light. It can illuminate the darkest corners and show us who we are and what we have to do in the clearest possible way. Without light, love, life and liberty cannot exist.

Relax and centre.

Starting in your meadow, ground yourself there, then go up your mountain to your temple of light. Enter the temple, stand in the very centre of the building, and visualise a beam of light filling you with soul qualities such a joy, love, truth, and beauty. Realise that through these qualities, light permeates everything.

When you are ready, return to your meadow, then to your everyday consciousness, bringing some of this light with you. Make sure you really ground yourself in your meadow, then again when you return to your ordinary consciousness, for without grounding you may remain 'spaced out' and the energy of the light may dissipate.

As you have already learned, the best way to ground anything is through expressing it. How can you express light in your life, right now? It may not seem obvious at first how you can do this, but if you remember how light permeates everything you do, you will find that any act performed with this consciousness can help manifest and ground light.

The following affirmation or 'prayer' connects you with the energies of love, life, liberty and light as you are able to experience them in your subtle and physical bodies. Using this affirmation opens the channels in your energy centres or chakras for the influx of soul energy. You can create a magnetic pull towards love, life, liberty and light through using this exercise to bring these energies into all parts of your being.

THE LIGHT BEARERS AFFIRMATION

I was conceived with love,
I was born to life;
I have grown in liberty,
I am a bearer of the light.

May all beings be blessed
with Love, Life, Liberty and Light.
Aum-Ha.

The following directions will help you effectively and easily connect with the energies evoked through this affirmation.

Before using the affirmation, relax and centre. Do the exercise standing up straight and erect but not rigid.

As you say 'I was conceived with love', with the forefinger

of your left hand touch your genital area, visualise your conception and the colour blue.

As you say 'I was born to life', touch your solar plexus or upper belly, visualise your birth and the colour green.

As you say 'I have grown in liberty' touch your heart, visualise your self as being strong and radiant with liberty, and the colour yellow.

As you say 'I am a bearer of the light' touch your forehead and visualise your whole being as infused with a strong white light.

Focus on these four centres and the colours there, then move to the next phrase. As you say 'May all beings be blessed. . .' hold your hands out before you as if blessing the world, and let the white light you are channelling flow from you into the collective consciousness. As you say 'Aum-Ha' bring your hands together in front of your chest and focus on yourself as a centre of consciousness and light.

You can do this affirmation alone, with other people, aloud, subvocally, in imagination; you can do it occasionally or often. It works well if you perform it at 'daybreak' (that is, at whatever time you first wake up, which is your own 'personal daybreak').

Imagine what it would be like if couples, pairs or threesomes of friends, groups of people of every kind, all over the planet, started performing this affirmation regularly. It would create a network of love, life, liberty and light over the whole planet.

Are you willing to partake in such a network of energy? What can you do to manifest and perpetuate this network?

Relax and centre.

Standing up with a straight but not rigid back, draw energy up from the ground through your body. Feel it energising you with strong, grounded strength. Imagine you have roots, like a tree, that extend deeply into the earth, holding you firmly in place.

Tune into your heart as a point of light in the middle of your chest.

Imagine a line of energy extending from your heart down into the ground and up, through your head, into space. Visualise this line of energy as a shining, silver light.

Imagine a second line of energy extending from your heart, this one going straight out in front of you and behind you, extending into space. Visualise this line of energy as a shining, silver light.

Continue to visualise these two lines of energy extending from you, up and down, forwards and backwards, so that they form a cross of light coming from the heart of your body and extending into infinity.

Visualise yourself as surrounded by a deep blue aura in the shape of an egg. On the surface of this aura are flashing golden stars. Take time to really visualise yourself as clothed in this blue egg.

Listen inside your awareness for the sound of a bell. When you hear it, allow its sound to fill you with a healing energy that makes you whole and strong.

Step forward into your future with confidence and connection.

Ritual

Ritual is so important in our lives, for when it is consciously performed with love and attention it charges up our energy on all levels. On the other hand, when ritual becomes habitual and loses consciousness and intention, it walls us in and stops us moving forward with the natural flow of our personal and collective evolution.

Consciously performed, ritual provides us with a way of ordering our experience organically, allowing us to connect our experiences into a larger whole, the total pattern of our unfolding life. Through ritual we can find new, larger meanings that help us evolve into new, larger beings, each time slightly further along the path of evolutionary change that leads us forward into our awesome but exciting future.

The Sanskrit root of the word 'ritual' is 'rita' meaning both art and order. It is the purpose of ritual to connect the art of our living with the order of our consciousness so that the two become one. When you order your life in this way, when you are truly centred, channelling energies from the soul and orchestrating your experience and expression, then you accumulate personal power. This personal power enhances the energy in your various subtle bodies and you become noticeably brighter to others, even if only unconsciously.

Rituals may be classified into two types, personal and group ones. Group ritual contains individual ritual, through the group being composed of individual participants. Individual ritual contains group ritual, for each individual is made of an 'inner group' of sub-personalities, or parts of the personality. Just as a group performing rituals must be in harmony for the ritual to work effectively, so this equally applies to the 'inner group' of subpersonalities. There is a need for both individual and group ritual, one being dependent upon the existence of the other just as a star (the individual) is dependent upon the galaxy (the group) and vice versa. Individual harmony may be achieved through ritual, which aids the inflow of transpersonal energies or soul qualities into the person. This is the uniting of the microcosm, or inner temple, with the macrocosm, or outer temple.

A group does not need to be led by any particular participant or 'leader'. Indeed, it is the 'power' of such leadership that so often leads to the corruption inherent in the organisations formed by various eastern 'gurus' and western 'masters'. The 'synthesising centre' of a group should rather be its common purpose, centred upon a symbol, object or belief that clearly enshrines and depicts this shared purpose. While a person can be such a 'symbol', the dangers of this are all too apparent.

For a group ritual to be effective there has to be a common, shared group purpose and a common, equally shared group endeavour. An effective group is not held together by a leader but by a common purpose, intention and plan. A group is like a solar system, where the planets are the members of the group and the sun is the common purpose. Grouped around the common purpose, the planets follow their course, the common intention, and thereby achieve the common plan, which is the manifestation of an active and growing system. In no way is their individual role in the whole scheme negated.

A group is a temporary aid to growth and seeing it in this way allows fuller commitment as it removes the fear for the individual of 'losing' identity except on a temporary basis. A group may be composed of any number of people, even only two. It is not the number of people in the group that makes it effective or not, but rather the quality of the work performed.

The most important elements for a successful ritual are good will, dynamic energy and focus or common purpose. A ritual needs to include the whole group in all these aspects, and the five main techniques that can be used to achieve this are love, meditation, sharing, communication and silence.

The Mystic and the Magician

There are two basic ways of changing consciousness which, although in essence are really one, are usefully described separately to help us gain a better understanding of their interaction and ultimate interdependence. These two ways are those of the mystic and the magician.

The mystic wants to change him or herself, to transcend the 'conflicts' inherent in everyday existence, and to do this attempts to rise up to the realm of potential (to transcend duality). The magician starts from the same place of wanting change to occur, but instead of choosing to transcend, chooses to draw the transpersonal, transformative energy down to the realm of the actual, to the world itself (to transform conflicts rather than transcend them). The magician's way is, therefore, one of the immanence which complements the transcendent way of the mystic. Each is necessary to the other.

Why incarnate and choose to have all the conflicts of life so that your soul can grow through learning how to deal with duality and the material plane, then spend your time here finding ways of leaving the world? If you have chosen to be here in the first place then what better than to reaffirm this choice and act upon it through action? The 'mystical trap', of avoiding conflicts, can be overcome, and the pain of life faced through making a clear identification with the soul.

It is so important now that we learn to differentiate clearly between owning and relinquishing responsibility. As part of the collective consciousness of life we are responsible for our environment, and so long as we avoid this we are unable truly to connect with our future potential.

The soul is like a projector, the source of light. All our potential for action is like the light that emanates from this projector. The world, the material life we exist within, is then the screen on which this light is projected. As a soul we are in contact with our Purpose, and we control the picture that is projected. That is our primary responsibility, that when we identify with the light source, we do not dwell in its truly magnificent presence, but we learn to share its energy with others through what we project on to the world, our screen.

Relax and centre.

Imagine a world in which everyone is a mystic, there is only love and no will.

Then imagine an opposite world, where everyone is a magician, and there is endless will but no love.

Finally, imagine a third world which combines the two, where people connect inwardly with love when it is appropriate, and where they use their will appropriately for experience and expression. In this third world there is a dynamic union between the archetypes of love and will.

It is possible to get 'gifts of energy' from your unconscious.

Relax and centre.

Starting from your meadow, travel to your mountain temple, and find within it a gift from the self. Whatever this gift is, bring it back to the meadow, then (symbolically or in actuality) do something that helps share your gift with the world.

Going up the mountain to the top is mysticism; bringing energy back down is magick. Learn to develop the direction with which you feel less connected, and to refine the one to which you already have a stronger connection.

Wealth

'Wealth' can be defined as the outcome of changes in the environment that are of benefit to humanity and/or other life forms on an individual or collective basis. By this definition, examples of wealth include a bridge across a river, a chair, a pollution-free environment, and so on. They would also include less tangible forms of wealth such as knowledge, understanding, warmth, joy, and so on, which, despite being non-physical, are none the less the most important items of wealth.

In an earlier chapter, we introduced a little-used word, coined by John Ruskin, namely 'Illth'. It is the opposite of 'well-th' and describes changes in the environment that are detrimental, for instance the existence of nuclear weapons, the use of gases that are destroying the ozone layer, non-biodegradable substances, and so forth. It also includes less tangible, but no less real, examples such as hate, envy and revenge.

Money should not be confused with wealth, or illth. It is a token, ticket or talisman used for the transfer of either wealth or illth. Unfortunately, many of our society's concepts and actions are built upon money rather than wealth. With our planet in its current state of crisis, environmentally, socially and politically, it is our clear moral duty as conscious beings to hold as many concepts and to make as many actions as we possibly can to encourage the growth of wealth.

Becoming Whole

The parts of anything may be put together to make a whole. Each 'whole' may then be put with other 'wholes' to make a greater 'whole', and so on to infinity. Before we can synthesise our inner parts in this way, however, we need to make each part whole in itself or the process of synthesis cannot be successfully accomplished. Hence the importance of continued personality work for every individual, at whatever level of 'evolution' they may be.

Each whole is always greater than the sum of the parts that make it up. There is something in the energy of the parts coming together to synthesise that unleashes a creative energy that can be utilised by the conscious individual. Although this organic process cannot be pushed or hurried, you can facilitate it through connecting with your soul as already described. Our work is in balancing and then synthesising all the opposites within and around us. The primary opposites we have to deal with are the archetypes of Love and Will and their manifestation through dualities such as male and female, anger and forgiveness, lust and power, spirituality and sensuality, idealism and practicality, toughness and sensitivity, discipline and spontaneity, freedom and order, intuition and logic. The important point to keep in mind at all times is the absolutely essential need for both parts of any duality.

Each of us creates our own mythology of opposites. There then can be situations where only one of the pair of opposites is obviously manifest, the other being underdeveloped or repressed. For example, you might be very obviously a loving person but not at all wilful (as far as can be obviously seen). Alternatively, there can be a direct 'here and now' conflict between any two opposites – for example, between a feeling you have to go for a walk and your thought that it is too cold outside.

It is possible to hold both opposites through an inclusive act. Yes, I will go out and I will wrap up warm. Yes, I will use an aerosol and I will ensure it is an environmentally safe one. An act of will, the taking of a direct choice is always the key, choice not as 'either this or that' but moving to a place outside the original opposites which can include both, then moving back into the situation with clearer awareness.

To solve a problem at its own level is impossible: you always need to move to a separate, 'observer' place from where, with a clear perspective, you are able to make the correct choice.

Relax and centre.

Identify two opposing parts in yourself, or parts in a current conflict situation, and listen to the voice of each concerning what they want and need at this time.

Move to the clearest inner space you have available to you, look back upon these two parts and their wants, consider what each needs, then ask yourself: 'what would it be like if these two parts came together?'

Act appropriately upon this.

The same process can be used to deal with conflicting 'parts' on a global level as well as on this individual level. Try this exercise again, but this time choose a current world conflict. See if you can really identify with the opposing forces and hear the voice of each. See the point of view of each side. Then move to a new, third position outside the conflict and ask the question: What would it be like if these two parts came together? You might not be able to get a complete picture or a total answer, but what you do understand in this way can help resolve the conflict, and you will now be able to send out a positive energy pattern that adds to the healing of the conflict.

We do not need to make a goal of some kind of perfection that we can never reach anyway. Instead we can accept constant change, and realise the energy in conflicts is the energy of the soul. We can also realise that all distinctions, including that between the soul and the personality, are illusionary. Such an attitude can give us flexibility in fulfilling our needs.

Relax and centre.

Recall three good, positive experiences from the last year or so and consider what were the common qualities in these three separate events. What made them positive rather than negative, desirable rather than objectionable, 'good' rather than 'bad'?

Although the distinctions between the experiences we call 'good' and those we label 'bad' are truly illusionary, from the point of our direct experience we sense them as good and bad. We can therefore clearly and consciously choose to move towards the good, those experiences that enhance our lives and bring wealth to us as individuals and to our environment.

Relax and centre.

Holding your arm out in front of you, move your hand in the air in a circular motion.

The hand is clearly real, but the circle is not, it is something you create in your mind. But is that hand itself so real? It is composed of atoms around which elements continuously create invisible circles. This, too, is in your mind.

There is nothing you cannot perceive, and nothing you can perceive that cannot be.
Infinity is implicit in every perception.

Relax and centre.

Tune inside and watch the flow of thoughts, feelings and sensations within your internal world. Be aware they are happening because you have chosen to be alive.

Open your eyes and look at the objects in the space around you and be aware they are there because you perceive them to be there. Realise this is true of the room or place you are.

Close your eyes and stay with this experience, then expand beyond this consciousness, beyond the room to the surrounding countryside, the country, the continent, the planet, the whole solar system, the milky way, our universe. All these things exist because you exist, and you exist because they exist.

Let your consciousness continue expanding outward to the totality of your reality. Imagine your consciousness as a point of light shining out over the whole universe.

Become aware there are other people and other beings in the universe. Each of them, too, is a point of light shining out over the whole universe. Sense the interaction between their experience and yours. See how this interaction creates a larger reality, a web of consciousness.

Now make a sound from your universe that harmonises with your sense of this totality. Recognise this one reality and choose to move towards it, this one reality that is being continuously created exactly as you choose it.

Slowly bring your consciousness back to our solar system, planet, continent and country. Turn your attention gradually to the room you are in, then the body you inhabit.

Be aware of the space you occupy, then open your eyes, right here and now, and see this one reality you create.

This is it!

Bibliography and Further Reading

Books can help us acquire both knowledge and understanding about ourselves and other people. If we read in a positive and active way, it can facilitate our growth. This involves reading slowly, stopping at times to reflect and evaluate, copying or underlining important sections, reading with attention and interest, and being willing to stop when tired or bored. If we read in this active way it strengthens our concentration and our will, and may even help us grow spiritually.

The following is not a complete bibliography but is a list of books you may find interesting and relevant if you have enjoyed this book. They can act as a starting point for further study and research into esoteric psychology and associated subjects.

Alli, A. *Angel Tech*, Falcon, 1986.
Alli, A. *All Rites Reversed*, Falcon 1987.
Assagioli, R. *The Act of Will*, Wildwood, 1973.
Assagioli, R. *Psychosynthesis*, Turnstone, 1975.
Assagioli, R. *The Laws and Principles of the New Age*, MGNA, n.d..

Bach, R. *The Bridge Across Forever*, Pan, 1985.
Bach, R. *Illusions*, Pan, 1978.

Crowley, A. *Magick*, Weiser, 1974.
Castaneda, C. *Tales of Power*, Penguin, 1976.

Castaneda, C. *The Fire From Within*, Century, 1986.
Capra, F. *The Tao of Physics*, Fontana, 1976.

Dychtwald, K. *Bodymind*, Wildwood, 1978.
Douglas, N. and Slinger, P. *Sexual Secrets*, Hutchinson, 1979.
Donner, F. *The Witches Dream*, Pocket, 1985.
Dali, S. *The Secret Life of Dali*, Vision, 1976.

Eastcott, M. *I, The Story of the Self*, Rider, 1976.

Ferrucci, P. *What We May Be*, Turnstone, 1982.

Garfield, P. *Creative Dreaming*, Future, 1976.
Grant, K. *Images and Oracles of Austin Osman Spare*, Muller, 1975.
Griscom, C. *Ecstasy is a New Frequency*, Bear, 1987.
Griscom, C. *Time is an Illusion*, Fireside, 1988.
Gibran, K. *The Prophet*, Heinemann, 1980.
Grof, S. *Beyond the Brain*, NYUP, 1985.

Houston, J. *The Search for the Beloved*, Tarcher, 1987.

Kenton, L. *The Joy of Beauty*, Century, 1983.

Leary, T. *Exo-Psychology*, Starseed, 1977.
Lowe, A. *Bioenergetics*, Coventure, 1975.

Mariechild, D. *Motherwit*, Crossings, 1981.
Masters, R. *The Goddess Sekhmet*, Amity, 1988.

Parfitt, W. *The Living Qabalah*, Element, 1988.
Perls, F. *Gestalt Therapy*, Penguin, 1973.
Perls, F. *In and Out of the Garbage Pail*, Bantam, 1977.

Redgrove, P. *The Black Goddess*, Bloomsbury, 1987.
Rogers, C. and Stevens, B. *Person To Person*, Condor, 1967.
Rosenburg, J. L. *Body, Self and Soul*, Humanics, 1985.
Reich, W. *Character Analysis*, Farrar, 1949.
Rilke, R.M. *Selected Poetry*, Picador, 1987.
Robbins, A. *Unlimited Power*, Fawcett, 1986.
Sharaf, M. *Fury on Earth*, Hutchinson, 1983.

Shuttle P. and Redgrove, P. *The Wise Wound*, Paladin, 1986.
Starhawk *Dreaming the Dark*, Beacon, 1982.
Stevens, J. *Awareness*, Bantam, 1976.

Tart, C. *Waking Up*, Element, 1988.

Wilde, S. *The Force*, Wisdom, 1984.
Wilson, R.A. *The Illuminati Papers*, Sphere, 1980.
Wilson, R.A. *Prometheus Rising*, Falcon, 1983.
Wilson, R.A. *The New Inquisition*, Falcon, 1987.
Wilson, R.A. *Coincidance*, Falcon, 1987.

INDEX